the green teen

the
eco-friendly
teen's **guide**
to saving
the planet

the
green teen

www.g2ggreen.org

Jenn Savedge

NEW SOCIETY PUBLISHERS

CATALOGING IN PUBLICATION DATA

A catalog record for this publication is available
from the National Library of Canada.

Cover design by Diane McIntosh

Printed in Canada. First printing March 2009

Paperback ISBN: 978-0-86571-649-0

Inquiries regarding requests to reprint all or part of *The Green Teen*
should be addressed to New Society Publishers at the address below.

To order directly from the publishers,
please call toll-free (North America) 1-800-567-6772,
or order online at www.newsociety.com

Any other inquiries can be directed by mail to:
New Society Publishers
P.O. Box 189, Gabriola Island, BC V0R 1X0, Canada
(250) 247-9737

New Society Publishers' mission is to publish books that contribute in
fundamental ways to building an ecologically sustainable and just society, and
to do so with the least possible impact on the environment, in a manner that
models this vision. We are committed to doing this not just through education,
but through action. This book is one step toward ending global deforestation
and climate change. It is printed on Forest Stewardship Council-certified
acid-free paper that is **100% post-consumer recycled** (100% old growth
forest-free), processed chlorine free, and printed with vegetable-based, low-
VOC inks, with covers produced using FSC-certified stock. Additionally, New
Society purchases carbon offsets based on an annual audit, operating with a
carbon-neutral footprint. For further information, or to browse our full list
of books and purchase securely, visit our website at: www.newsociety.com

NEW SOCIETY PUBLISHERS
www.newsociety.com

Recycled
Supporting responsible use
of forest resources
www.fsc.org Cert no. SW-COC-1271
© 1996 Forest Stewardship Council

CONTENTS

IT'S YOUR PLANET, TOO!

Global warming, air pollution, water pollution, deforestation, endangered species...these are the issues that are affecting our planet today. They are problems that, if left unchecked, could completely disrupt the way people live on this planet. Global warming in particular has the potential to wreak havoc on the planet as we know it.

The good news is that there are actually a lot of things that each and every one of us that shares this planet can do to reverse these dangerous trends and make our world a safer, healthier, and more balanced place to live.

As a teen, you may think that there is nothing you can do to save the planet. But that is just flat out wrong. There are hundreds of things that teenagers can do...in fact...there are hundreds of things that teenagers, just like you, *are doing right now* to protect the environment.

Let's face it...it is your generation that is really going to feel the effects of the environmental issues that are building today. Adults will not see the devastating effects of global warming that you and your children and your children's children will have to face head on. So while it's all well and good to enlist the help of adults in the environmental movement, it is really you and your generation that need to spearhead the charge to change.

Teens have the knowledge, the skills, and the POWER to save the planet. Use this book to show you how.

WHAT YOU CAN DO ABOUT GLOBAL WARMING

The Scoop: The greenhouse effect is a natural process whereby gases in the Earth's atmosphere trap radiation from the Sun and keep the planet warm. The greenhouse effect is a GOOD thing...without it...the planet would be about 60°F colder. The problem is that over the years we humans have sent too many extra gases into the atmosphere, and too much of the Sun's radiation is being trapped and sent back to Earth...warming the whole planet (hence, the name Global Warming). The temperature has already risen to a point where it is affecting the earth's climate.

The Cause: There are a number of human and natural activities that release greenhouse gases into the atmosphere. The worst offender is the burning of fossil fuels like oil and coal (in factories, cars, power plants, etc.). Deforestation is another major cause of global warming as trees soak up greenhouse gases when they are alive but release them when they are cut down or burned.

The Effect: Even the slightest increases in temperature can have a drastic effect on the planet. Higher temps have already caused glaciers in the Arctic to melt, resulting in the loss of habitat for many animals as well as a rise in sea levels. If global warming continues unchecked, it can cause extreme weather conditions (droughts, floods, heat waves, hurricanes, and blizzards), a rise in the incidence of tropical diseases, and changes to the world's agricultural seasons. All of these effects can add up to

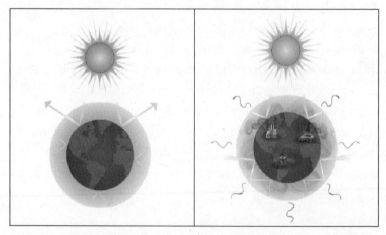

Under normal conditions, the greenhouse effect keeps the planet nice and warm

Human activities like manufacturing, driving, and deforestation send too many gases into the atmosphere, increasing the global temperature to dangerous levels.

some serious problems for the economy and dangerous consequences for the health of humans, plants, and animals on the planet.

The Fix: The gases that are in the Earth's atmosphere now, and the ones that are being pumped out today, will remain in the atmosphere for the better part of the next century. So global warming will happen...and it is likely that you will see some of its effects your lifetime. But it is still possible to ensure that those effects don't become catastrophic, if we act now. Politicians have been arguing about global warming for years... without solving anything. The time has come to stop counting on politicians and start reversing this dangerous trend. Here's how:

1. Use Less Energy...in your home, at school, and on the go
   * Don't Drive (Chapter 5)
   * Flip The Switch (Chapter 7)
   * Shorten Your Shower (Chapter 8)
   * Put On A Sweater (Or Take One Off) (Chapter 7)
   * Hold The Beef (Chapter 2)

2. Plant A Tree...
   * At Home (Chapter 2)
   * At School (Chapter 13)
   * In Your Community (Chapter 15)

GREEN
YOURSELF

Want to go green? Start with yourself. You may not realize it but the decisions you make everyday, from what you have for breakfast, to what you will wear to school, to how you spend your free time, all affect the planet. The food you eat, the clothes you wear, the books you read, the games you play, and even the text messages you send all require energy, use resources, and create pollution.

Fortunately, there are a ton of simple things you can do each and every day to make the world a better place. By making smarter decisions about the items you buy, the food you eat, the clothes you wear, and the way you get around, you can significantly reduce your environmental impact and improve your chances of getting others to do the same. You have the power to make the change. Use it!

AT THE STORE

Did you know that kids influence the spending of $300 billion a year, or about 1 in 3 consumer dollars spent? That's why corporations target *you* to buy their products. And you may not realize it, but almost everything you buy can affect the environment. Fortunately, there is now a green option for just about any item on your shopping list. Using your green to buy green protects the planet, promotes fair treatment for workers, and sends a powerful message to businesses about the importance of environment. But the key is to know how to spot the eco-gems from the phonies. Here's what you need to know to shop green:

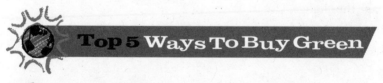

Top 5 Ways To Buy Green

1 **The 24 Hour Rule:** Keep the planet in mind when you are shopping and ask yourself if you *really* need each purchase. Can you get by without it? Is it possible to rent, borrow, or swap with a friend instead? If you really want it, try the 24 hour rule. Give yourself one day to think it over and if you still want it...go back and get it.

2 **Learn Your Labels:** Green labels are splashed on almost every product in the store. But beware...some of those labels may be just a meaningless attempt to get you to spend your money. Don't be fooled. Check out the tips in this chapter to learn which labels to look for when shopping.

3 **Buy In Bulk:** Save money and the planet by purchasing items in bulk whenever possible. Buying in bulk is cheaper than purchasing several smaller items and it will minimize the amount of packaging that you need to toss.

4 **B.Y.O.B.:** (Bring Your Own Bag) Plastic shopping bags are lame! They use a ton of petroleum based resources (contributing to global warming) and create a ridiculous amount of litter and waste. Pick up a snazzy, compact, reusable tote bag and carry it with you to hold your purchases.

5 **Buy Recycled:** Look for stuff that contains recycled content (to save on new materials.) There are lots of eco-friendly products now, from pencils to notebooks, jackets to sneakers, and even dog beds that contain recycled material. Purchasing these products reduces the consumption of new materials, reduces landfill waste, and supports the market for recycling.

Why Bother?

Every item you buy affects the planet in one way or another, whether it's the clothes on your back that are made with pesticide laden crops; the hamburger on your plate that required a slew of energy, land, and grain to produce; or the cell phone in your pocket that may be made with illegally mined minerals that endanger animal habitat. The good news is that you have the power to choose what and how much you will consume. By using less stuff and selecting eco-friendly products you can make a huge difference in the impact your shopping will have on the planet.

g2g Green Tips

Minimize Packaging

It's hard to buy stuff that doesn't come layered in packaging... boxes, plastic, bubbles...you get the picture. Look for items that use the least amount of packaging or packaging that you know you can reuse.

Buy Local

After you check the label to see if your new found bounty is eco-friendly, check to see where it was made. Organic clothing that is shipped across the world will create enough pollution to negate its environmental benefit. Look for the Made in the USA label, and when possible, look for products that are made as close to your home as possible.

At The Store

Avoid Non-Recyclable Packaging

Choose products in containers that are easily recyclable. Check out Earth 911 (**earth911.com**) to find out what and where to recycle in your area. If your local center doesn't accept it, (for example, #5 Plastic) try to avoid buying it.

Skip Disposables

Disposable products take a toll on the environment twice. They use resources and create pollution and waste first in their production and again every time you have to return to the store to replenish your supply. Choose reusable versions of batteries, pens, cameras, coffee mugs, silverware, plates, etc.

Don't Get Greenwashed!

Green is "in," and big manufacturers know it. Unfortunately, some companies try to cash in on the green movement by labeling their products with meaningless propaganda that may make it look eco-friendly, even when it's not. This is called greenwashing.

Here's a quick list of the labels to look for (the ones that mean a product is the real green deal). In the following chapters, look for the "CHECK YOUR LABELS" box to help you sort out the green from the greenwashed.

**USDA Certified
Organic (Food)**
*Organic Label courtesy
of USDA AMS

**Leaping Bunny:
(Cosmetics,
Personal Care and
Household Products)**

**FSC Certified
(Wood, Paper Products,
and Furniture)**

**Energy Star
(Appliances)**

**Fair Trade Certified
(Food, Clothing,
Wood Products)**

Be A Label Lover

Want to know what all those labels really mean? Here's a quick and dirty guide to the green, the bad, and the ugly...

Look for these labels:

Cradle 2 Cradle: Cradle 2 Cradle certification analyzes the environmental impact of a product throughout its entire life cycle. Products that use this label are made with eco-friendly materials, are designed for reuse, use energy and water efficient technologies, and are produced under socially responsible conditions. The certification is found on a wide range of products from cleaning agents (Begley's Best) to surfboard wax (Wet Women Surf Wax).

Energy Star: There are more than 50 different types of products (battery chargers, dehumidifiers, ceiling fans, dishwashers, televisions, cordless phones, computers, printers, and even windows and doors) that can apply for the Energy Star label. The products that do wear it use less energy and less water than comparable models.

Fair Trade Certified: The Fair Trade label can be found on foods such as coffee, tea, chocolate, rice, sugar, and bananas to indicate that the items were produced under fair working conditions. When you see this label on a product, you'll know farm workers got a fair price for it, children were not forced to make it, and a limited number of chemicals were used in its production.

FSC (Forest Stewardship Council) Certified: The Forest Stewardship Council certifies wood and wood products that come from sustainable forests. Look for the FSC label on wood, paper, and wood products such as furniture, cabinets, and windows.

Greenguard: The Greenguard Environmental Institute is a non-profit organization that certifies products with low or no indoor emissions (and therefore fewer harmful chemicals). Look for the Greenguard label on building materials, furniture, household cleaning products, electronic equipment, and personal care products.

Green Seal: Products labeled with the Green Seal minimize their environmental impact from manufacturing to disposal. Look for this label on paper, wood products, household cleaners, and personal care products.

Leaping Bunny: Look for the Leaping Bunny logo on cosmetics, personal care products, and other household products and you will know that it has not been tested on animals, nor does it use animal products in its ingredients.

Organic: Foods labeled organic (such as fruits, vegetables, meat, poultry, and dairy products) must be produced without the use of synthetic pesticides and fertilizers, antibiotics, genetic engineering, irradiation, and sewage sludge. Animals raised for organic meats must have access to the outdoors and must be fed 100% organic feed that does not contain animal byproducts or growth hormones. However, the USDA draws a distinction between chickens and other animals. So cows that are raised to produce organic beef or milk must have continuous access to the outdoors without confinement, whereas chickens are not guaranteed access and can be confined.

There are three different organic labels that you may see on the shelves:

100% Organic: Products bearing this label can only contain organically produced ingredients.

Organic: Products can use the "Organic" label if 95% of their ingredients are organically produced and the remaining 5%

are non-organic ingredients that have been approved by the National Organic Program.

Made With Organic Ingredients: This label means that the product is made with at least 70% organic ingredients, at least three of which are listed on the back of the package. The remaining 30% of ingredients can be non-organic but they must be approved by the National Organic Program.

Processed Chlorine Free: Look for the PCF label on paper products to make sure they are processed without the use of environmentally damaging chlorine.

Rainforest Alliance Certified: This is similar to the FSC label.

Don't Get Greenwashed!
Beware of these labels:

Biodegradable: This is a popular greenwashing label, but in reality it means nothing. Most products will biodegrade, or break down, eventually, but that doesn't mean they are eco-friendly. In addition, there are no independent agencies that certify this label as accurate.

Cruelty-Free: Unless this label is accompanied by the Leaping Bunny label (see above) it doesn't mean a thing. This term is not legally defined and there is no agency that verifies the claim.

Free Range: The "free-range" label brings to mind animals roaming free in an open pasture, grazing in clean fields and drinking from fresh, cool streams. Unfortunately, this is rarely the case. For starters, the US Department of Agriculture has only defined the term for labeling poultry, not beef or eggs. So a "free range" label on eggs is completely meaningless. And the vague wording of the definition makes it meaningless for poultry as well. According to the regulations, in order for poultry to be labeled "free range" the chickens must "have access to the outdoors for an undetermined period each day." This means that having the coop door opened for a mere 5 minutes each day is good enough to get a stamp of approval from the USDA (even if the chickens never saw that it was open).

Non Toxic: "Non-toxic" is another pointless label that is neither legally defined nor certified.

Recyclable: Just because a product is labeled "recyclable" does not mean that you will actually find anywhere to recycle it. Contact your local recycling center to find out what products and materials are accepted in your area.

Recycled: The term "recycled" is legally defined by the US Federal Trade Commission (FTC) however, it is not verified by the FTC or any other agency. So what's the point? Another problem with this label is that the FTC does not distinguish between pre-consumer and post-consumer waste. Post-consumer waste has already been used at least once and returned to the waste stream (i.e., yesterday's newspaper). Pre-consumer wastes, such as shavings from a paper mill, have never been used. Your best bet is to look for products that uses the highest percentage post-consumer waste possible.

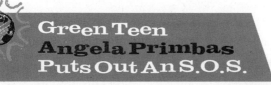

Green Teen
Angela Primbas
Puts Out An S.O.S.

As a kid, Angela Primbas loved to play in the stream behind her house. So when she learned that is was becoming polluted, along with the entire watershed feeding nearby Lake Erie, she decided to do something about it. Here's how Green Teen Angela Primbas put out an S.O.S. to save the planet.

Angela Primbas, 18, has been working to clean up water pollution since the 7th grade.

Q: *When did you first learn about that pollution in Lake Erie?*

A: When I was a kid, I can remember seeing a sign that was posted on one of the beaches at Lake Erie that said the beach was closed to swimming because of pollution. That was a big wake up call for me. I also learned about pollution in my 7th grade science class. Environmental issues weren't really part of my school's curriculum, but I was lucky enough to have a science teacher that really cared about the environment and shared with us some facts about pollution. Between those two avenues, I learned about the toll that pollution is having on our community.

The Green Teen

Q: *Why did you decide to get involved?*

A: Two friends who were in that science class with me were also really concerned about what they were hearing. So we got together and founded a group called Save Our Stream (S.O.S.). We were really concerned about non-point source pollution which is essentially a form of pollution that can't be traced back to any one source. It comes from the entire watershed. We were interested in figuring out where this came from and what we could do to stop it.

So we did a little bit of digging and research and found out that there was a certain type of fish called the Native Ohio Brook Trout that is becoming endangered because of this non-point source pollution. This fish is one of the only native fish to our area and it's only found in Ohio. If we lose it here, then it's gone forever. If this fish dies out then the entire food chain… all of the streams and rivers…gets thrown off balance. Other species will die as a result of it. The entire cold water ecosystem would essentially be destroyed by this pollution.

So that's where my friends and I decided to start. We first learned about pollution while we were sitting in the classroom and then we saw its effect first hand on a stream that ran right past my house that had brook trout in it. We wanted to stop this from happening because this is one of our unique natural species that you can't get back once it's gone.

At The Store

Q: *How did you get started?*

A: With S.O.S. we decided to tackle the problem of the native brook trout dying out because of pollution, using two general methods: First, is education. Non-point source pollution comes from everyday people like you and me using too much fertilizer, washing their cars with the wrong types of detergent that run into the stream, littering, and all sorts of activities that most people don't realize will have a big impact. But they actually do have a big impact. Over the course of S.O.S.'s five years in existence, we've presented educational programs to over 3000 people, from kindergarten students to high school seniors. We've presented symposiums and handed out pamphlets to let people know that pollution is a big problem and it's everyday people like us that are the source of it…not some far away factory.

Second, we also work on community preservation efforts. We design projects to get the community involved and basically restore areas of land or vegetation near a stream that were depleted. We help to restore areas of vegetation called riparian buffers that are next to streams that act as a natural filter for runoff and non-point source pollution. We've also had several tree planting events. In 9th grade we took our freshman class out to plant trees. Most recently I took middle school students from four different middle schools in my community out to plant a rain garden (an area of vegetation near a stream that filters rainwater before it gets into the lake. These projects not only help the environment, but they also get students involved in preserving it.

Q: *What has been the most difficult part of your efforts to clean up the environment?*

A: I've worked with some really great people over the years that have been more than willing to help and to listen to what I have to say. But I've also run into people who don't want to listen to me because they think I'm too young to know what I'm talking about. I've had people ask me before, *"Why should I listen to you? What authority do you have to tell me where pollution comes from and what we can do to stop it? Where is your PhD?"* So the biggest obstacle I faced was that some people had these prejudices and they wouldn't listen to what I was saying because they were so focused on the fact that I haven't gone to college yet because I'm only 17.

But on the other hand, a lot of people are thrilled to hear about environmental issues from a fresh, young voice. Teachers especially love it when we request to go into classrooms and give presentations or organize events with the kids. They like to see young people getting other young people involved in preserving the environment.

Q: *What advice do you have for other teens who want to launch a similar project?*

At The Store

A: My best advice? Don't let anything stop you. I was at a college interview the other night and I was describing one of the environmental projects that I work on to keep non-point source pollution and invasive species out of Lake Erie. The interviewer responded by saying that he thought my project was pointless because invasive species are just going to get into the lake anyway. My response to him was that no, I don't believe it's just going to happen anyway, especially if we can educate boaters to clean out their ballast water so there is less of a chance that an invasive species can be transferred from one body of water to another. I was so surprised that this guy would just completely criticize everything I was doing and everything I believe in.

So even if you're faced with this kind of criticism, you can't let it stop you. There are going to be people who don't want to listen and there are going to be people who don't want to take what you're saying very seriously. But if it's something that you really believe in, you have to just go for it. When you do you'll find that there are a lot of people out there that want to help you, especially if you're young, because they are thrilled to have bright new energy involved in the environmental movement.

To learn more about non-point source pollution, check out the S.O.S. website (**saveourstreams.org**) or the Lake Kleenerz website (**lakekleenerz.org**) that highlights Angela's efforts to clean up Lake Erie.

GetYour Parents Involved

* **Be Their Guide:** Save your parents time and money by researching their green shopping options for them. Canvas local stores and scour the web to find sources for green goods and then compile your research into a buying guide for your family. Check out The National Green Pages (**greenpages.org**) and Responsible Shopper (**responsible shopper.org**) to get you started.

* **Do The Math:** If you want your folks to spend their hard earned money on eco-friendly stuff, you may need to show them the math on how these products will either:
  A) Save them money over the long run (as is the case for CFL bulbs) or
  B) Remarkably save the planet.

* **Do The Math:** Show your parents that you've really thought about what you're asking them to do. And if necessary...

* **Take The Hit:** If it is going to cost $20 more each week for your parents to buy organic groceries at the store, offer to absorb the costs by paying for them with your allowance or giving up something you've been begging for but don't really need. Make it a family effort so that your parents will know how important this is to you.

Sites to Surf

The Coalition For Consumer Information On Cosmetics	(888) 546-CCIC info@leapingbunny.org Info about the Leaping Bunny Label **leapingbunny.org**
Earth Island Institute	(415) 788-3666 For more information about the campaign for Dolphin-Safe tuna **earthisland.org**
Forest Stewardship Council	(877) 372-5646 info@foreststewardship.org **fsc.org**
I Buy Different	Info about the economic, environmental, and social pitfalls of consumerism **ibuydifferent.org**
MBDC	Cradle 2 Cradle Certification (434) 295-1111 info@mbdc.com **mbdc.com**
National Marine Fisheries Service	Information about the Dolphin Protection Consumer Information Act **nmfs.noaa.gov/**

The Rainforest Alliance	(212) 677-1900 info@ra.org Information about the SmartWood Program **rainforest-alliance.org**
Responsible Shopper	Research a company's environmental and social impacts before you make your next purchase. **coopamerica.org/programs/rs**
The Consumer's Union Guide To Environmental Labels	A comprehensive guide to environmental labeling on food, personal care products, household cleaners, and paper products **greenerchoices.org/ecolabels**
TransFair USA (TFUSA)	(510) 663-5260 transfair@transfairusa.org Information about Fair-Trade Certification **transfairusa.org**
United States Department of Agriculture (USDA)	National Organic Program (202) 720-5115 nopwebmaster@usda.gov **ams.usda.gov/nop**
US Environmental Protection Agency	Energy Star Program (888) STAR-YES **energystar.gov**

2

EATING YOUR GREENS

It used to be when your mother told you to eat your greens, she was talking about spinach and broccoli. But greens have grown up, and teens now have access to an assortment of "green" foods that are better for your health and that of the planet. From vegetarian burgers to organic coffee, it's never been easier or tastier to eat your greens. Here's the scoop:

Top 5 Ways To Eat Your Greens

1 **Buy Local:** Did you ever think about where your food comes from and how far it has to travel to get to your plate? Even produce that is grown organically will cause unnecessary environmental damage if it must be flown from overseas, or trucked across the country to get to your kitchen table.

Opt for local in-season foods whenever possible. (Check out Sustainable Table (**sustainabletable.org**) for a list of produce available by state and season.

2 **Buy Organic:** Organic foods are better for the planet because they are produced without the use of any pesticides or genetically modified ingredients. They are safer for the environment, safer for farm workers, and better for your health. But not all organic foods are made the same. Keep reading to find out the best foods to buy organic.

3 **Hold The Beef:** It takes a heck of a lot of land, water, grain, and pesticides to raise a cow. And cows are a significant source of methane (which contributes to global warming). The average American eats 4 servings of beef a week. Skip the beef in just one meal a week and you'll reduce your environmental impact by 25%.

4 **Skip The Fast Food:** Sure, it's tempting, but fast food is a disaster for your health and the planet. If you need something quick, grab a PB&J, heat up a can of soup, or toss together a veggie wrap to take with you.

5 **Compost the Leftovers:** Toss your leftovers in the compost pile instead of the garbage can. Composting will keep food scraps from filling up landfills and turn them into a usable product that's great for your soil. See page 28 to learn how to start your own compost pile.

Why Bother?
In a word: Pesticides. It takes about 300 different pesticides to grow the fruits and vegetables that stock grocery store shelves.[1] These chemicals can harm your health, pollute the environment, and negatively affect fish, birds, and other wildlife. Pesticides are also dangerous for the farmers who are exposed to them on a daily basis. The Environmental Protection Agency (EPA) estimates that pesticides are responsible for 20,000–40,000 work-related poisonings each year in the United States.[2]

g2g Green Tips

Go Veggie

A vegetarian diet is not only healthier for you, it is also better for the environment. Producing fruits and vegetables is exponentially easier on the environment than raising beef, pork, or poultry. Don't be intimidated. You don't need to completely give up meat to make a difference. Try it for just one day each week and you'll significantly reduce the amount of water, energy, and land needed to fuel your diet. Think cheese pizza, mac and cheese, or spaghetti with tomato sauce to get you started.

Green to Go

If you're eating out, look for restaurants that use local and organic foods in their selections. Check out the Eat Well Guide (**eatwellguide.com**) for a list of restaurants that use local, sustainable ingredients. Try to minimize waste by using the minimum amount of paper napkins and plastic silverware and cups. If you need to get something to go, like a cup of coffee, be sure to carry a reusable mug to minimize the waste.

Don't Fall for Free Range

The free-range label is basically meaningless (see Chapter 2), so don't be greenwashed into purchasing products that carry it.

How To Start Your Own Compost Pile

Compost is the ultimate recycler, turning your yard waste and kitchen scraps into usable mulch that you can use to feed your plants. It's as eco-friendly as you can get. And the best part about it is that it is cheap, and after the initial set-up it is relatively easy to do. There are many resources you can turn to to learn more about composting, but here are the basics:

1. A successful compost pile needs two basic components: carbon (shredded newspapers, cardboard, and straw) and nitrogen (lawn clippings, kitchen waste, and weeds).

2. Combine these components in a ratio of roughly 5 parts carbon to 1 part nitrogen in a compost bin or pile in your yard.

Eating Your Greens

Feeling lazy? Leave the pile alone and you will have usable compost by next year. In a rush? Turn the pile and add a sprinkle of water every few weeks and your compost will be ready in about three months.

When To Buy Organic

Foods that carry the certified organic label are made with less chemicals and genetically modified ingredients than their conventionally grown counterparts. However, they also cost more and may be more difficult to find. Get the most eco-benefit for your time and money with the following guidelines on when to buy organic:

Always: Apples, bell peppers, celery, cherries, imported grapes, lettuce, nectarines, peaches, peanut butter, pears, potatoes, red raspberries, spinach, and strawberries.

When Possible: Beef, poultry, and eggs.

Don't Bother: Onions, avocado, pineapples, mango, asparagus, kiwi, bananas, cabbage, broccoli, eggplant, and seafood.

One final note: All grocers are legally required to place organic foods (especially fruits and vegetables) where they won't be exposed to the pesticide-laden water runoff from conventional produce. If your local store has forgotten that rule, remind

them. If they still don't move the organic food, shop some-
where else.

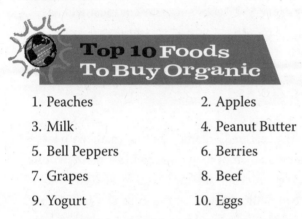

Top 10 Foods To Buy Organic

1. Peaches
2. Apples
3. Milk
4. Peanut Butter
5. Bell Peppers
6. Berries
7. Grapes
8. Beef
9. Yogurt
10. Eggs

Need this list on the go? Text BUYORGANIC to 4-INFO
(4-4636) to get it sent to your cell phone.

Check The Labels

Look for these labels when you shop for organic foods. See
Chapter 1: Green Shopping Tips for label definitions.

Get Your Parents Involved

* **Plan The Menu:** Offer to plan (and even cook) tonight's dinner to show your parents how yummy green foods can be.

* **Get Growing:** Talk to your folks about starting a small garden this year so that you can grow some of your own herbs and vegetables. If your family doesn't have the time or space for a garden, try growing salad greens, cherry tomatoes, or herbs in a window box.

Sites to Surf

Local Harvest	(831) 475-8150 **localharvest.org**
Sustainable Table	(212) 991-1930 info@sustainabletable.org **sustainabletable.org**
United States Department of Agriculture (USDA)	National Organic Program (202) 720-5115 nopwebmaster@usda.gov **ams.usda.gov/nop**

GREEN YOUR WARDROBE

A generation ago, eco-friendly clothes were hideous (itchy burlap shirts, tie-dyed shirts, and shapeless dresses). But teens today are in luck because eco-fashion is all the rage and green clothes can be found in every shape, size, style, and color. There is also a greater selection of "pre-loved" clothes at thrift stores, on Ebay, and in consignment shops that help you look good while you save money and the planet.

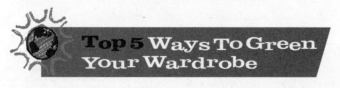

Top 5 Ways To Green Your Wardrobe

1 **Fix It**: Need something new to jazz up your wardrobe? Try taking a fresh look at what's in your closet to see what can be fixed and what can be reconfigured into something great.

Green Your Wardrobe

Learn how to sew a button or patch a hole (or make a hole); or re-tailor worn out duds by turning last year's pants into shorts or an old dress into a skirt.

2 **Consider "Preloved"**: Most thrift stores are a treasure trove of amazing clothes in every shape, style, and color. "Pre-loved" duds save money and reduce the use of new materials while keeping the old items out of the landfill.

3 **Seek Out Organics**: When you have to buy new, look for clothes labeled 100% organic. Cotton, linen, wool, bamboo, and hemp can all be grown organically and used to produce green clothing.

4 **Keep It Fair**: A $5 t-shirt may seem like a great deal, but you have to remember the environmental and social costs required to make this garment so inexpensive. Look for clothing that has been independently verified as "sweat-free." (See What You Can Do About Sweatshops for more info.)

5 **Give Them A Second Life**: Don't toss your clothes in the trash. If you can't use it, and none of your friends want it, pass it on to a local charity or thrift store. If it is simply too worn out, cut it up to use as rags around the house.

Why Bother? You probably don't think
of pesticides when you think of your clothes, but did you know

that ¼ of all the pesticides used throughout the entire world are used in the production of cotton. Not for food crops like soybeans, or rice, or wheat, or potatoes, but for cotton. Conventionally produced clothing is heavily laden with other noxious chemicals too (like formaldehyde) in dyes and finishes. And to keep clothes cheap, many items are produced using child labor forces in deplorable sweatshop conditions.

g2g Green Tips

Buy To Last

Buy high-quality clothes that are made to last instead of flimsy, cheap garments that will probably fall apart after the first washing. Give hems and seams a tug to check for sturdy stitching; inspect the fabric to make sure it is strong; and test patches and appliqués to make sure they are sewn on well.

Swap It

Update your wardrobe, hang out with your friends, and help save the planet by hosting a clothing swap. Ask everyone to bring a bag of gently worn duds to exchange for another at the party. You can also check out a Swap-O-Rama-Rama (**swapo ramarama.org**) event in your area. In addition to clothing swapping, these events also host sewing and fashion workshops so that you can learn to get the most from your wardrobe.

Green Your Wardrobe

Rebuild Your Clothes

Look for clothing manufacturers, like Patagonia, that collect worn-out clothes and rebuild them into new garments. Under Patagonia's Common Threads Garment Recycling Program (**patagonia.com/recycle**), customers can turn their worn out fleece and t-shirts into next year's clothing line.

Don't Get Taken To The Cleaners

It's a huge hassle and waste of money to take clothes to the dry cleaners, so steer clear of clothes that require such treatment. If you absolutely have to have something dry-cleaned, look for a shop that uses greener methods such as wet-cleaning or liquid CO_2 to reduce its toxic load.

Sponsor A Princess

Non-profit organizations like The Princess Project and The Glass Slipper have helped thousands of high school girls feel like Cinderella on prom night by providing free gowns, jewelry, and accessories. Why not pass on your dress when prom season is over?

It Isn't Fair!

How fair is the clothing produced at your favorite college? Check out United Students Against Sweatshops (**students againstsweatshops.org**) to protest unfair labor practices used to make university clothing.

Check The Labels

Look for these labels when you shop for eco-friendly clothing. See **Chapter 1** for label definitions.

100% Organic

Get Your Parents Involved

* **Fix Their Fashion Faux Pas:** Improve your parents embarrassing wardrobe by pointing out the eco-friendly fashions that will fit their style (and maybe even improve it a bit!)

* **Help Them Dress For Success:** Tell your folks about Dress for Success (**dressforsuccess.org**) a national organization that collects and distributes professional business clothing, shoes, and accessories to women around the country.

Sites to Surf

Sustainable Clothing Information:	
Lotus Organics	Offers in-depth information about sustainable clothing and organic fibers **lotusorganics.com**

Green Your Wardrobe

Clothing Donations Sites	
Goodwill Industries International	**goodwill.org**
Soles 4 Souls	Collects gently used shoes for children and adults in need **soles4souls.org**
Teens For Jeans	**teensforjeans.com**
The Glass Slipper Project	Collects and distributes prom dresses and accessories in the Chicago area **glassslipperproject.org**
The Princess Project	Collects and distributes prom dresses and accessories in the San Francisco Bay area **princessproject.org**
The Salvation Army	**salvationarmyusa.org**
Anti-Sweatshop Resources	
Co-op America	**sweatshops.org**
United Students Against Sweatshops	**studentsagainstsweatshops.org**

4

GET SQUEAKY CLEAN AND GREEN

The next time you're in the bathroom, take a close look at the products you slather on your body, hair, and face. The toxic ingredients found in many personal care products are bad for you and awful for the environment. And there is very little information about what exactly happens when all of these chemicals and synthetic ingredients mix together in your body, in the air, in the soil, and in the water supply.

The good news is that you don't have to give up washing your hair or smelling good in order to protect your health and be nice to the planet. There are safe, non-toxic alternatives to virtually every personal care product you need. Here's how to get squeaky clean and smelling sweet without loading up on chemicals.

Top 5 Ways To Go Green While You Get Clean

1 **Read The Labels:** Steer clear of any personal care product that contains one or more of these ingredients: phthalates, mercury, toluene, lead, formaldehyde, petroleum distillates, parabens (hormone-disrupting preservatives such as methylparaben, butylparaben, ethylparaben, isobutylparaben, and propylparaben), or BHA. These chemicals are the worst offenders to your health and that of the environment. (To have this list sent to your cell phone, text BADCHEMS to 4-INFO.)

2 **Get Skimpy:** Try using a little less of your personal care products to stretch your dollars and reduce the chemicals in your body and in the environment.

3 **Don't Be Cruel:** Animal testing is unnecessary, unethical, and just plain cruel. Look for the "Leaping Bunny" label to make sure your beauty products have not been tested on animals. (See Chapter 1 for the definition of the Leaping Bunny label.)

4 **Wipe That Carbon Footprint Off Your Face:** You probably know that the use of petroleum is a primary contributor to global warming. But did you ever realize how many petroleum-based products are hiding in your bathroom vanity in the form of lip balm, lotions, lubricants, and even plastic covered sanitary products. Pass on products that use petroleum or its derivatives (paraffin oil, propylene glycol, and ethylene) and look for alternatives such as beeswax, cocoa butter, and vegetable oils instead.

5 **Skip Disposables:** According to the environmental news website Grist (**grist.org**), 2 billion disposable razors end up in United States landfills each year.[3] Invest in a reusable and refillable razor to save money and take a knick out of waste.

Why Bother? Consider these frightening facts:

* 89% of the 10,500 ingredients used in personal care products have not been evaluated for safety by the FDA, the Cosmetic Ingredient Review (an in-house panel appointed by the cosmetics industry), or anyone else.[4]

* A 2004 survey by the Environmental Working Group, a nonprofit research group, found that the average adult uses approximately nine personal care products each day, for a total of 126 unique chemical ingredients.[5]

* While some products are tested for reactions such as skin redness, rashes, or stinging, there is little to no information about the long-term safety of these chemicals when they are mixed together, either in your body or in the environment.

Get Squeaky Clean and Green

Conventionally-produced personal care products fill your body and the environment with chemicals. Nothing could be less beautiful!

Go Au Natural

Look for cosmetics and personal care products that use organic and all-natural ingredients. Hint: you should be able to pronounce (and even eat) any ingredient on the label!

Smells Like Teen Spirit

Many products that are supposedly "fragrance-free" actually contain "fragrance" as an ingredient as well as additional masking fragrances that give the product a neutral odor. If you are looking for a fragrance-free product, scrutinize the label and make sure the term "fragrance" is not listed as an ingredient.

Be Mild To Dry Skin

If your skin is chronically dry, try using a milder soap that is gentler on your skin. Soap is made to remove dirt and grease from your skin, but harsh, abrasive soap may also remove too much of your skin's natural oils, creating the need for you to use an additional product. Look for a milder soap that can reduce dryness naturally.

DIY

Got some extra time and ambition on your hands? Consider making your own personal care products. Check out *Naturally Healthy Skin: Tips & Techniques for a Lifetime of Radiant Skin* by Stephanie Tourles, or click on My Beauty Recipes (**mybeautyrecipes.com**) for recipes for everything from shampoo to mouthwash.

Hit The Spa

A day out at the beauty salon should leave you feeling clean and beautiful, not laden with toxic chemicals. Find out which products your local hair or nail salon uses and ask if they will use organic hair and skin care products upon request.

Get Your Parents Involved

* **Give Them An Update:** Are your folks still using the same brand of shampoo and conditioner they used when *they* were teens? Give their beauty regimen an update with info about all of the great health and environmental benefits of using natural and organic products.

Get Squeaky Clean and Green

* **Beauty In A Bottle:** Mix up a batch of pampering, all-natural lotion for your mom or clean, eco-friendly shower gel for your dad. Check out My Beauty Recipes (**mybeautyrecipes .com**) for ideas.

Check The Labels

Sites to Surf

Compact For Safe Cosmetics	Download a list of companies that have pledged to keep personal care products "cruelty-free." **safecosmetics.org**
The Consumer's Union Guide To Environmental Labels	Detailed information about the labels on your favorite personal care products. **greenerchoices.org/ecolabels**
Skin Deep Environmental Working Group	A comprehensive campaign to inform consumers about the toxins in personal care products. **cosmeticsdatabase.com**

5

GREEN GIVING

You don't have to leave your conscience at home the next time you head out to buy a gift for a friend or family member. There are plenty of gifts that you can give for any occasion that are both perfect for the recipient and gentle on the environment. Here's how to find green gifts for everyone on your list.

Top 5 Ways To Give Green

1 **Tempt Their Tummies:** Everybody needs to eat, right? Edible gifts such as cookies, organic coffee, or fresh flowers make a thoughtful gift for almost any occasion and produce very little waste. And besides, who doesn't love a batch of gooey, fresh baked cookies or a delicious cup of organic, fair-trade hot chocolate?

2 **Be A Slave:** Save cash and reduce waste by offering up your services in lieu of a material gift. Offer to baby sit, shovel snow, clean a room, make dinner, develop a website, weed the garden, wash the dog, or run an errand (the possibilities are endless).

3 **Give A Service:** Give a gift certificate for a no-waste service such as a massage, haircut, or housecleaner.

4 **Be Charitable:** What do you buy for the friend who has everything? Consider donating to a charity that is near and dear to the recipient's heart. Check out the Charity Navigator (**charitynavigator.org**) to find a charity to match anyone's interests.

5 **It's A Wrap:** Regular wrapping paper costs a bundle and lasts but a few minutes before it hits the trash bin. Consider using a green alternative such as a reusable bag or basket, a scarf, or recycled materials such as newspaper or brown paper bags. You can make your package beautiful with natural adornments such as flowers, dried berries, or pine cones. If you need to mail the package, replace plastic bubble wrap and Styrofoam peanuts with eco alternatives such as crumpled newspaper or empty egg cartons.

Why Bother? The gifts you give affect
the Earth in the resources they use and the waste they create.

But more importantly, they are a reflection of who you are as a person and how you choose to honor your friends and family. Green giving lets you celebrate birthdays, holidays, and other special occasions in eco-savvy style.

g2g Green Tips

Turn Up The Green

Keep the environment in mind when you purchase gifts by looking for fair-trade, organic, or locally grown options whenever possible. If it's appropriate, consider giving a gift such as a solar powered battery charger or a basketful of compact fluorescent light bulbs to get a friend started on the eco-path.

Make It Yourself

If you have the skills, consider making a handmade gift that is much more likely to be cherished (and retained) by the receiver. Put together a scrapbook, make a photo frame, or sew an apron for an easy low-impact gift.

Buy Local

Look for gifts that are produced close to home. Whether it's a basket of fresh vegetables from a local farm or a ceramic bowl made by a local potter, locally produced gifts minimize the emissions and packaging involved in shipping.

Green Giving

Buy Preloved

Hit your local thrift shop, flea market, or vintage boutique to find a wide range of unique and time-tested gifts. If necessary, refurbish the item with a new coat of paint or a well placed ribbon to turn it into a gift the receiver will treasure.

No-Waste Gifts

Gift cards to a favorite restaurant or store are easy to give and popular to receive. Other no-waste gift ideas include tickets (movies, theater, or sporting events), club memberships, or charitable donations.

Offset Them

Carbon offsets are another great no-waste gift that actually help to save the planet. For every dollar you spend on Renewable Energy Credits (RECs) or carbon offsets, money is donated to support a renewable energy or tree-planting project, thereby "offsetting" your friend's carbon emissions. Check out Carbon Neutral (**carbonneutral.com**) or Green Tags USA (**greentagsusa.org**) to calculate carbon emissions and purchase greentags.

Unplug

Try to avoid giving gifts that will continue to produce waste or require electricity. If you have to give a power-hungry gift, throw in a package of rechargeable batteries and a charger to eliminate waste.

Give Green Toys

Look for FSC-certified wood and organic fabrics when choosing green toys for kids. And when you have to go with plastic, steer clear of soft plastic toys that are likely to contain polyvinyl chloride (PVC). The European Union recently banned the sale of toys containing PVC after studies found that these toys leached phthalates that may disrupt the natural development of hormones.

Celebrate Green Holidays

Every year, Americans send out 7 billion greeting cards, use more than 38,000 miles of ribbon and throw away over $300 million in wrapping paper during holiday celebrations. Of course, no one wants to be Scrooge, or be forced to give up their favorite family traditions, in order to go green. But there are plenty of ways to celebrate with style without wreaking havoc on the planet. Here's how to celebrate your favorite holidays with green spirit.

Christmas/Hanukkah/Kwanza

- Decorate with eco-savvy bling such as low-energy lights or a reusable menorah or kinara.

- Skip the paper cards and send e-cards to friends and family.

Green Giving

* Use old maps or the Sunday comics to wrap gifts or use gift bags and decorative boxes that can be reused from year to year.

* Compost your Christmas tree or Kwanza mazao and vibunzi

* Save bows, ribbons, holiday cards, and other decorations to reuse next year.

Easter

* Buy eggs at your local farmer's market, or purchase organic eggs from the store.

* Shred scratch paper or old magazines to use as "grass" in your basket in place of the plastic variety. After the holiday, reuse the grass again for packing material or compost.

* DIY your DYE by using natural foods such as onion skins (yellow or red), beets, spinach, blueberries, coffee, tea, turmeric, or paprika to dye your eggs.

Halloween

* Need a costume? Raid the thrift store or host a costume exchange party to trade costumes with friends.

* Hand out healthy treats to your trick-or-treaters, such as fair trade chocolates, organic raisins, individually-sealed bags of microwavable popcorn, and all-natural snack bars; or give out non-food items such as stickers, soy crayons, or temporary tattoos.

Valentine's Day

* Save the paper and send your loved one a mushy e-card

* Show your love (for your beau and the planet) with organic flowers or chocolates.

How To Throw An Eco-Savvy Party

A green party is a great way to let loose, hang out with friends, and celebrate your efforts to save the planet. Here's how to make sure your next bash is earth-friendly.

Invites: Save money and resources by sending invites via email or text message. If you need to send an invitation by snail mail, make sure it is printed on recycled paper.

Decorations: Skip the paper and plastic and decorate with natural items from your backyard such as plants, flowers, and pinecones. Pick up reusable decorations such as pillows, scarves, and other fabrics.

Party Supplies: If possible, use reusable dishes, utensils, and cloth napkins. If you do need to use paper products, seek out those made from compostable materials or the highest recycled-paper content possible. Rent or borrow items that you won't need more than once like insulated beverage containers or large serving dishes.

Green Giving

Gift Bags: If you're handing out party favors, replace the bags of gift junk with eco-friendly gifts such as consumables (cookies, plants, or flowers) tickets (sporting events, movies, museums), or reusables (picture frames or art supplies).

Food: Avoid waste by thinking conservatively when planning how much food to serve and be sure to donate any extra non-perishable items to your local food shelter.

Trash: Set up recycling areas near your trash cans so that guests can easily recycle cans, paper, and glass.

Get Your Parents Involved

* **Throw A Party:** Help your parents organize an Eco-Savvy Potluck Party with your friends and family. Ask guests to bring dishes prepared with local and organic ingredients so you can socialize, swap recipes, and share eco-treats.

Sites to Surf

Care2 Greenliving	25 Great Consumer-Less Gift Ideas **care2.com/greenliving/25-great -consumer-less-gift-ideas.html**

Grist, Environmental News and Commentary	grist.org
Sierra Club Green Gift Ideas	sierraclub.org/e-files/gift_ideas.asp
The Natural Resource Defense Council Great Green Gift-Giving Guide	nrdc.org/cities/living/ggift.asp
Treehugger	treehugger.com

GREEN
ON THE GO

Why is it, that despite 20 years of innovation, gas mileage has just barely improved over the last 20 years? In 1987, the average fuel economy of cars and light trucks peaked at 22.1 miles per gallon; twenty years later (in 2006), the average fuel economy for passenger cars hit 21 mpg.[6] It's no wonder that cars are such a huge contributor to global warming! The time has come to reverse this trend. Here's how to green your ride.

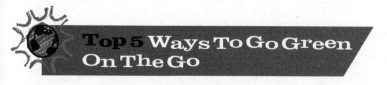

Top 5 Ways To Go Green On The Go

1 **Don't Drive!** One of the very best things you can do to save the planet is to drive as infrequently as possible. Take public transportation, walk, or bike whenever you can. Even if you only do it once in a while, you will save money, decrease the wear and tear on your car, reduce pollution, and reduce your contribution to global warming.

2 **Buddy Up:** Pair up with friends and classmates to share rides to work, school, and after-school events. You'll save money, save the planet, and maybe even make some new friends.

3 **Be Smooth:** Drive smoothly to get the most out of your fuel economy. Avoid jackrabbit starts, aggressive driving, and hard braking.

4 **Stay In Tune:** A tune-up will keep your car operating at its maximum efficiency, emitting fewer pollutants and sucking down less fuel. Whether you do it yourself or go to a mechanic, be sure your car is checked for worn spark plugs, dragging brakes, and low transmission fluid. Replace your air filter as necessary and be sure your wheels are properly aligned and rotated.

5 **Pump 'Em Up:** Keep tires properly inflated to reduce wear and tear on the tread and save fuel over the long run. Check your owner's manual for the recommended inflation level (this number is also usually printed inside the door frame of your car).

Why Bother?
Global warming is no joke. It is real and it is happening and guess what…cars are a huge part of the problem. According to a recent report from Environmental Defense, the transportation sector is responsible for about one-third of the US's total production of carbon dioxide, a major contributor to global warming.[7] Tame your travel and you will significantly reduce your environmental footprint.

g2g Green Tips

Multitask
Planning ahead to combine trips when possible will save time, money, and energy (yours!). A cold engine pollutes up to five times more than one that is warmed up. So combining several short trips into one can make a big difference for the planet.

Lighten Up
If you've got a bunch of junk cluttering up your trunk or back seat, you could be wasting gas and adding to your carbon footprint (or tire print?) It takes about 100 extra pounds to reduce your fuel economy by 1%. So, if you just have a few extra text books rolling around, don't sweat it. But if you are carting around an array of sports gear and instruments, it might be time to clean it out.

Ban American "Idles"

Newer cars do not have to be warmed up like older models, so
there is no need to allow you car to idle in the driveway any-
more. Turn off your ignition any time you will be stopped
or parked for more than a few minutes. If you live in a cold
weather climate use a reflective windshield shade in the winter
to reduce frost and save time and energy on the scraper.

Park It

When you park, protect your car from the elements and it
won't have to work as hard to heat up or cool down. In the
summer, park in the shade or use a reflective windshield shade
to keep your car cool and reduce fuel evaporation. If you have
access to a garage, use it. It will keep your car cool in the summer and warm in the winter.

Maintain Your Ride

Take care of your car and it will take care of you and be gentler
on the planet. Regular maintenance and tune-ups, changing
the oil, and checking tire inflation extend the life of your car,
reduce the incidence of break-downs, improve gas mileage, and
lighten the load on the planet.

Green Your Oil Changes

It's a good idea to change your car's oil and oil filters regularly
to improve fuel economy and keep your car running smoothly.
If you do it yourself, be sure to recycle the oil properly and fill

up your engine with clean recycled motor oil. Plug your zip code into the Earth 911 website (**earth911.com**) to find a used motor oil drop-off location near you. If you take it in to a service station, make sure that they will do the same.

Pump Smart

Don't "top-off" your car at the pump. Overfilling by even a little bit can lead to pollution-causing gas spills. When possible, get fuel when the weather is cool to minimize evaporation and prevent gas fumes from heating up and creating ozone. And look for gas stations that use pollution-reducing vapor-recovery nozzles (those thick, accordion-looking plastic devices covering the gas nozzle).

Clean Car Washing

Commercial car washes use about half of the water it takes to wash your car at home. Newer shops use high-pressure, low-flow nozzles to minimize water and energy usage, and some even recycle their greywater to further reduce water consumption. Washing your car at home not only wastes water, it also sends a bucket load of soap suds, gasoline, and exhaust residue directly into storm drains and waterways.

Need a fundraiser? Instead of the traditional car-washing fundraiser, see if your local car wash will sponsor your club or sports team for a day (giving your group a percentage of the profits for the folks that stop by and drop your name). Or check out Chapter 11 for more green fundraising ideas.

Two-Wheeled Fun

Get out your bike (the non-motorized kind) and ride it. Use your bike instead of your car to get to school and work, run errands, and meet-up with friends. You will save a fortune in gas money while you're saving the planet!

Make Your Own Green Car

It's not as hard as you may think to turn any old jalopy into an eco-friendly ride. Consider converting your existing gasoline motor to electric or biodiesel or even building your own eco-friendly car from scratch. Bart Grabman did it...see how he did it below.

Renting and Sharing

If you need to rent a car, look for a company that offers eco-cars as part of their line-up. Better yet, check to see if there is a car sharing option, like Zipcar or Flexcar that would fill the need.

Planning An Eco-Friendly Vacation

Whether you're headed off on a family vacation or a spring break road trip with your friends, here's how to go green and relax with a clear conscience.

* **Before You Leave:** Save energy by taking a few minutes to unplug appliances, computers, power strips, and televisions before you leave your house. Adjust your thermostat so that

you are not heating or cooling an empty house (just be sure to leave the house a comfortable temperature if pets are staying behind).

* **Go Local:** Consider visiting local attractions, like the newest exhibits at a nearby art museum, aquarium, zoo, or botanical garden. Go rock climbing at a local park or gym or see the wildlife at a state park. Mark your calendar for special events like concerts, art shows, food-and-music festivals, book readings, and more.

* **Consider Traveling by Train:** Planes emit more carbon dioxide per traveler than any other means of transportation, followed by cars and trains. Save the planet and travel by train for your next vacation.

* **Minimize Waste:** If you're staying at a hotel, be sure to reuse your towels to save both energy and water. Turn off the television and lights, and adjust heat or air conditioning settings if you'll be gone for the day. Pack a reusable drink bottle to refill with clean water. And pack your own toiletries rather than using the hotel's mini bottles.

* **Buy Sustainable Souvenirs:** Why bother purchasing t-shits or tacky knick knacks that have been imported to your destination when you can buy locally produced souvenirs that offer a pleasing memory of your trip? Locally produced foods, crafts, art, or jewelry support the community and reduce the pollution and transportation costs associated

with importing goods. Do not buy souvenirs made from endangered species, hardwoods, or ancient relics.

* **Go Digital:** If you don't already have one, look for an inexpensive digital camera to capture your vacation's highlights. If you take a lot of pictures, you will easily recoup the costs of the camera in film and processing fees.

How Green Teen Bart Grabman Made His Own Eco-Savvy Car

As a teenager living in Alaska and an avid skier, Green Teen Bart Grabman knows all about snow. And he could see first hand that global warming meant less snow and an earlier spring...in other words...terrible conditions for skiing. What Bart didn't know much about was cars; but that didn't stop him from taking on a project to convert a gasoline powered car to electric, reducing his overall contribution to the greenhouse gases that cause global warming. Here's what Green Teen Bart Grabman had to say about his electric Volkswagen Super Beetle.

Q: *What inspired you to build an electric car?*

A: I was taking a class at school called Pasages, and the purpose of the class was to take something that you're interested in and expand on it in some way. For instance, in the past, one student who had an interest in carpentry built a gazebo for students to enjoy during lunch. I had two interests that I wanted to expand upon. I wanted to do something to help the environment, and I wanted to learn more about cars. So I thought it would be interesting to combine the two ideas into one project. Building an electric car just seemed like a logical next step.

Q: *Is the car finished?*

A: I haven't finished it yet but it's pretty close. It still needs some minor wiring…I have 96 volts of car batteries to power it and I still need to wire this to the existing wiring that came with the car so that everything functions correctly. I've taken it out for short trips in front of my house, but it's not ready for longer trips yet.

Q: *How much did you know about cars before you started this project?*

A: I pretty much knew nothing about automotive technology when I started this project. But I've done a lot of learning. One good thing is that I choose a VW Super Beetle over a more modern complex car. This has been really helpful because it's relatively simple in terms of the mechanisms and the motor. The VW Super Beetle is pretty basic so it was a good place to start…especially with my lack of knowledge.

Q: *If you were to start this project again knowing what you know now, what would you do differently?*

A: I would have started with a different car. I know I said before that it was a good idea to start with a car that is simple. But the one that I got…well, it had seen better days. The floors were rusted out and the interior wasn't in good shape. I've had to spend a lot of time working on those types of things. I think if I'd chosen a better car to begin with, it would have been easier going.

Q: *What would you say has been your biggest obstacle in completing this project?*

A: Time and money. I'm a high school student, and I have a lot of stuff going on, so I don't have a lot of time or money to spare. But there have been a lot of people who have helped me out on this project in some way or another. So I've never had any trouble getting things done when I do actually work on them. But just finding that time is one of the hardest things.

Q: *What is the environmental issue that concerns you the most?*

A: I'd have to say global warming. Being from Alaska, where more than half the year here is snow, I've noticed more recently a decline in the snow levels. Springs are earlier and we have record breaking fires in the state every year because it's drier and the warmer temperatures bring more pests that kill the trees. Global warming is very evident here.

Q: *What advice do you have for other teenagers who are looking to try a project like this?*

A: Find something that you're interested in and don't be discouraged by setbacks because there will of course always be some setbacks…if not many. But the results will definitely outweigh the troubles. As long as you follow through, it's going to be a very rewarding experience when you're finished.

Get Your Parents Involved

* **Ask Jeeves:** Parents do make handy chauffeurs. But it's better for the planet to walk, ride your bike, or share rides with friends headed in the same direction. (Just make sure your parents know where you are and how you'll be getting home!)

* **Beat The Numbers:** Gas prices are at an all time high, so it's likely that your parents are already looking for ways to cut back on their gas guzzling. Help them figure out the gas mileage for the family car and suggest ways to make improvements. Here's how:

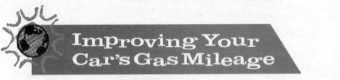

Improving Your Car's Gas Mileage

1. Reset the car's trip-o-meter the next time you fill up with gas.

2. At the next gas stop, record the total number of miles driven. Divide this number by the number of gallons required to fill the tank. This is your miles per gallon (MPG) or the number of miles you get out of each gallon of gas.

3. Continue recording your gas mileage in this way and use the tips above to beat these numbers.

• **See A Show:** Take your parents to a nearby car show to learn about the latest trends in eco-savvy cars and trucks.

TGT's Guide to Eco-Cars

Gasoline-Powered Eco-Cars: The majority of eco-cars on the road today are called partial zero-emissions vehicles (PZEVs) that run on gasoline but use other technologies to improve gas mileage and reduce pollutants (ie hybrids).

Pros: Emit fewer pollutants and use less fuel than their traditional counterparts

Cons: $$$$

Flexible Fuel Vehicles: According to the US Department of Energy (DOE), all gasoline vehicles are capable of operating on gasoline/ethanol blends with up to 10% ethanol. However, there are also millions of cars on the road known as Flexible Fuel Vehicles (FFVs), that can run on E85 (85% denatured ethanol and 15% gasoline). Is ethanol the fuel of the future? The jury is out but it doesn't look good.

Pros: Uses less gasoline

Cons: Difficult to find fueling stations, may be dated technology with social/economic/environmental costs of its own

Biodiesel: Biodiesel fuel is made from a combination of diesel and refined vegetable oil. It burns cleaner than straight diesel and produces fewer emissions. Biodiesel fuel can be hard to make, and even harder to purchase, but co-ops and service stations are popping up all over the country. You can also convert your engine to run on straight vegetable oil but this can be costly and difficult to accomplish.

Pros: Drastically reduces or completely eliminates the use of gasoline, smells like French fries!

Cons: Can be difficult/costly to convert cars to run on biodiesel, and even harder to find fuel

To Find A Biodiesel Fueling Station near you, Text NBIO + Zip Code to 4-INFO (4-4636)

Sites to Surf

Alternative Fuels Data Center US Department of Energy	**eere.energy.gov/afdc/**
Biodiesel America	(310) 496-3292 In-depth information on biodiesel **biodieselamerica.org**
Grassolean	**grassolean.com**
Green Car Congress	**greencarcongress.com**
GreenerCars.org **American Council for an Energy-Efficient Economy**	(202) 429-8873 info@aceee.org **greenercars.org**
Hybrid Cars	**hybridcars.com**
National Biodiesel Board	(800) 841-5849 info@biodiesel.org **biodiesel.org**

Green On The Go

Fuel Economy Information	**fueleconomy.gov**

US Environmental
  Protection Agency
Green Vehicle Guide
  National Vehicle and Fuel
  Emissions Laboratory
	(734) 214-4200
	greenvehicles@epamail.epa.gov
	epa.gov/greenvehicles

Veggie Van	Josh Tickell's Biodiesel Journal **veggievan.org**

WHAT YOU CAN DO ABOUT AIR POLLUTION

The Scoop: Air pollution occurs when solid particles and gases (or pollutants) get trapped in the air. Some air pollutants are bad for your health, as well as the plants and animals that we share the planet with. And if you think you can hide from air pollution by staying inside, think again, without proper ventilation, air pollution can be even worse inside your home and school.

The Cause: The main causes of outdoor air pollution are car emissions, the use of fossil fuels, gas emissions from factories, burning trash, the use of agricultural chemicals, wildfires, and landfill emissions. Inside, air pollution is caused by pollutants like radon and volatile organic compounds (VOCs) that are emitted from things inside your home, such as building materials, paints, new furniture, cleaning solutions, carpets, dry cleaning, and so on, and so on.

The Effect: Air pollution is terrible for your health. Once those minuscule particles get trapped in your lungs, they can cause or aggravate conditions like asthma, allergies, bronchitis, and lung and heart diseases. In the same way, air pollution is detrimental to the health of plants and animals. It also contributes to global warming and causes "acid rain" which can kill fish and tress and damage buildings and cultural resources (like artifacts). In areas with particularly filthy air, air pollution can affect visibility making it difficult for both humans and animals to get around.

The Fix: The best way to clean up your air is to stop doing and using the things that release pollutants into the air:

1. Don't Smoke: This is a no-brainer. Pollutants in cigarette smoke are nasty for your lungs and the planet.

2. Don't Drive (Chapter 6)

3. Ban Bus Idling (Chapter 11)

4. Buy Organic (Chapter 2)

5. Pump Smart: (Chapter 6)

6. Put Out The Fire (Chapter 7)

7. Speak Up (Chapter 15)

GREEN
YOUR HOME

Your home. It's where you live, where you sleep, and where you cross paths with the rest of your family. It's also the place where you share meals, toss your trash, plug in your computer, and grab a shower...in other words it's a place where you and your family use resources and create waste. The average American household consumes over 100,000 gallons of water, 13,000 pieces of paper, and 25 gallons of chemicals, while generating over one ton of trash per person and 11,200 pounds of air pollutants (including 22 tons of carbon dioxide) each year. Whew! Don't be fooled into thinking that pollution, global warming, and deforestation are only caused by big companies. The choices you and your family make in your home go a long way toward saving the planet. Check out these chapters to learn about the simple things you can do to green your home.

TRIM YOUR WASTE-LINE

Imagine going to your room only to find out that it has been filled with garbage. Now imagine that your whole house is overflowing with garbage. That is exactly what is happening on our planet! Each person in the US generates an average of 4.6 pounds of garbage each day. That means in this country alone, we are creating over 250 million tons of garbage each year!

Garbage, also known as municipal solid waste, is basically any item that gets thrown away rather than reused or recycled. Grass clippings, food scraps, broken toys, paper, old clothes, furniture, appliances, and batteries can all be found in the waste stream. But all of these items are also easy to reuse or recycle. Do your part to lighten the load on the planet and reduce the amount of stuff you throw away. Here's how:

Top 5 Ways To Trim Your Waste-Line

1 **Buy Less Stuff:** Do you really need that new shirt or those new gadgets? Think twice the next time you are at the store, because the absolute best way to reduce waste is to keep it from coming home with you in the first place.

2 **Go Paperless:** Paper makes up over ⅓ of the waste in the US, so do your part to reduce waste by going paperless. Ask your teachers if you can hand in assignments via email or on a reusable disk instead of on paper. Read news and magazines online, send texts instead of notes, and give e-cards to save both paper and cash.

3 **Don't Trash Your Lunch:** Is your lunch waste-free? Whether you bag it or buy it, make sure you don't trash it. (See below for tips.)

4 **Swap It:** Don't throw away your old stuff, swap it with a friend instead. You'll both get something new and your stuff will get a second chance at life.

5 **Recycle:** If you're not already recycling, get on it. Recycling makes a huge difference for the environment: it conserves materials, saves energy, prevents pollution, and reduces the need for new landfills.

Why Bother? Have you ever thought

about where all of your garbage goes once it leaves your house? Most of the trash in the US is sent to a landfill where it is essentially buried under layers of clay and topsoil. The problem is that these landfills take up a lot of space. According to the Environmental Protection Agency, the amount of trash generated in this country has more than doubled over the past 30 years, but the amount of space we have to throw it all away has remained constant. Some communities, especially those in congested areas, have to truck their garbage to neighboring towns, requiring more energy and resources (and creating more pollution) along the way. Reducing the overall amount of garbage we produce will alleviate other environmental problems such as global warming, pollution, and deforestation.

g2g Green Tips

Choose Reusable Over Disposable

Steer clear of disposable products such as coffee mugs, batteries, plates, cups, razors, napkins, and pens. Use reusable, rechargeable, or refillable products instead.

Consider "Preloved"

Consider purchasing a gently used or "preloved" item to keep it out of the landfill and reduce the need for new materials.

Trim Your Waste-Line

Go Back For Seconds

At the dinner table, get in the habit of taking smaller portions and going back for seconds if you are still hungry. This strategy will help keep you from wasting food (or packing on too many calories!).

Don't Buy It...Borrow Instead

Check out your local library or movie store to borrow books, movies, magazines, or music, instead of buying them.

Repurpose It

Keep your old stuff out of the trash by finding a new life for it. Repair, refill, rebuild, or otherwise re-purpose things instead of tossing them.

Turn Trash Into Cash

If it's worth something, you can make a tidy profit by selling clothes, toys, electronics, and books at a yard sale, consignment shop or on websites like Ebay (**ebay.com**) or Craigslist (**craigs list.org**). If that doesn't work, donate them to your local thrift store or use Freecyle (**freecycle.org**) to find someone in your area who might need them. One person's junk is another's treasure.

Turn Trash Into Art

Get creative by using old items (such as broken gadgets, torn clothing, or plastic bottles) as art supplies.

The Green Teen

Put Out The Fire

Burning trash releases pollutants and greenhouse gases into the atmosphere. So skip the fire and find ways to reduce the amount of trash you produce instead.

Flip It

Get the most out of each sheet of paper by using both sides in the printer and for notes, sketches, doodles, shopping lists, and phone messages.

See Double

Ask around at local schools, libraries, and museums, to see if any of your waste (such as jars, magazines, paper towel rolls, newspapers, or plastic bottles) could be used for art projects.

Close The Loop

Look for recycled content in the products that you buy. These products have reduced the need for new materials and lightened the load on landfills.

Weigh Your Waste

Every night for a week, collect your household garbage and weigh it on your bathroom scale. Record your results and celebrate your success as your trash slims down.

Trim Your Waste-Line

What (Why and Where) To Recycle

Currently, about 25% of the garbage in the US is recycled, but experts estimate that 65% of our garbage *could* be recycled. Recycling options vary by city or county. Most areas collect office paper, cardboard, magazines, newspaper, aluminum, plastics, glass (colored or clear), steel, yard trimmings, tires, batteries, and building materials. Use this chart to get a better idea of what you should recycle and why. Then check out Earth 911 (**earth911.org**) to find out where to send your recyclables. Once you have it all filled out, cut it out and post it on your fridge as a reminder to the rest of the family.

What	Why		Where
	What It Makes	What It Saves	
Aluminum	New aluminum cans	Uses 95% less energy to make a can from recycled materials than from virgin ore	
♻ **1** **PETE** PETE Plastic (Bottles for soft drinks, water, juice, liquor, cough syrup, tennis balls, and cleaning products)	New plastic containers, sweaters, shoes, luggage, upholstery, carpeting, fiberfill for sleeping bags and coats, and fabric for T-shirts and tote bags.	Manufacturing bottled water uses over 1.5 million barrels of oil per year. In one year, that's enough oil to fuel 100,000 cars.[8]	

What	Why		Where
	What It Makes	**What It Saves**	
♻ **2** **HDPE** HDPE Plastics (milk and laundry detergent bottles)	New bottles or plastic pipe.	47% of all plastic bottles used in the US are HDPE	
Newspaper	Newspaper	If all our newspaper were made from recycled paper, we could save about 250,000,000 trees each year!	
Corrugated Cardboard	Chipboard, boxboard (i.e., cereal boxes), paper towels, tissues, and printing paper	Uses about 75% less energy to make cardboard from recycled materials than from virgin pulp.	
Steel Cans	New steel cans	If we recycled all of our steel cans we would save 144 kilowatt hours of electricity, 63 pounds of coal, 112 pounds of iron, and 5.4 pounds of limestone.[9]	

Trim Your Waste-Line

What	Why		Where
	What It Makes	What It Saves	
Glass	New glass jars and bottles and fiberglass insulation.	Using recycled glass to make new glass requires 40% less energy than making it from virgin materials.	
Paper	New paper, molded packaging, compost, and kitty litter.	Paper products make up about 35% of the trash in the US (the largest single sector of waste.)	
Need this list on the go? Text RECYCLEIT to 4-INFO (4-4636).			

Get Your Parents Involved

* **Stop Junk Mail:** Show your parents how to stop junk mail from clogging up the mailbox. For unsolicited credit card offers, they can call 1-888-5 OPT OUT (or 1-888-567-8688) 24 hours a day. For the rest of the junk, check out **dma choice.org**, or send a postcard or letter to:

    Mail Preference Service
    Direct Marketing Association
    P.O. Box 643
    Carmel, NY 15012-0643

- **Bag It:** Stash a reusable bag in the car that your parents can use in place of plastic or paper bags whenever they make a purchase.

- **Start A Compost Pile:** Talk to your folks about starting a compost pile in your backyard to trim your trash and make your own all-natural fertilizer. (See Chapter 2 for more info on starting a compost pile.)

- **Give 'Em An I.Q. Test:** Challenge your parents to test their trash can I.Q. Click on **thegreenparent.com** and search for "Trash Can I.Q." for a fun test that will help your parents understand the impact of the trash they throw away each day.

SAVE YOUR ENERGY

Americans use nearly a million dollars worth of energy every minute...**EVERY MINUTE!!** A good portion of that energy is used in the home to power your laptop, heat your water, and keep your room a comfortable temperature. Reducing energy consumption in your home is easier than you think, and it can go a long way towards reducing the threat of global warming. Here's how to do it:

Top 5 Ways To Save Energy

1 **Put On a Sweater (Or Take One Off)**: Feeling cold? Don't reach for the thermostat, just put on a sweater (or take off a layer if you get too hot).

2 **Flip The Switch**: Make it a habit to turn off the lights if you're the last person to leave a room.

3 **Pull The Plug**: Unplug appliances and gadgets when you're not using them so that they don't burn energy in "standby mode." Major energy drainers include phone chargers, computers, televisions, extra refrigerators, and printers.

4 **See the Light**: CFL bulbs cost a few cents more than standard bulbs, but they require about ¼ of the energy to produce the same amount and quality of light, and they last ten times as long.

5 **Hibernate**: If you'll be away from your computer for an hour or more, turn it off. For shorter breaks, use the "Sleep" or "Hibernate" modes to reduce energy use and save the time it takes to reboot.

Why Bother? Wasting energy contributes
to global warming and pollution, damaging water resources, triggering acid rain, deteriorating human health, and damaging habitat for wildlife. Every kilowatt you conserve and every battery you save can significantly help to save the planet while reducing your family's monthly energy bill.

g2g Green Tips

Green Power to Go

Use rechargeable batteries instead of disposables to power your laptop, video games, PDA, cell phone, or iPod. Or check out the latest line of solar-powered chargers that harness the sun to juice up your gadgets without the waste.

Do Some Dusting

Another way to get the most from your light bulbs is to keep them clean and dust-free (dirty bulbs don't give off as much light.)

Get Cooking

Larger pots take a longer time to heat up (and use more energy in the process). Use the right size pot for the job to save both time and energy! And use the microwave to heat small stuff (like a bowl of soup or a cup of tea) to cut energy use by 75%.

Looking For Leaks

Energy leaks waste time, money, and valuable energy. Try these tricks to seal out leaks throughout your house:

Windows and Doors: Find a piece of ribbon and hold it near windowsills and at the base of doors on the next windy day. If it's fluttering, you have a leak. Simple steps like insulating, weather stripping, and installing storm windows can reduce your home's energy use by 20–30%.

The Fridge: Check the gaskets around your fridge to make sure they are clean and tight to lock in cold air. Here's the test: close a dollar bill in the refrigerator door with part of it sticking out. If it is difficult to pull out, the gaskets are sealing properly. If it pulls out easily, tell your folks it's time to replace them.

Hot Water: Take a quick look around your hot water heater to make sure that it is not leaking. Even a small drip of water can add up to a huge waste of both energy and water.

Check The Numbers

Check these appliances to make sure they are adjusted to the most energy-efficient setting:

* Water Heater: 120 degrees
* Thermostat: 78 degrees (summer) 68 degrees (winter)
* Refrigerator: 38 to 42 degrees (0–5 degrees for the freezer)

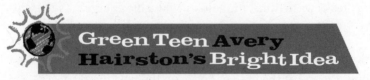

Green Teen Avery Hairston's Bright Idea

While adults are busy debating which laws, regulations, and tax incentives might one day help to reduce global warming,

Save Your Energy

The Teen Advisory Panel of Relight NY: (from left) Avery Hairston (founder), 16; Peter Ginsberg, 17; Brendan Harvey, 16; Peter Chapin, 17; Taiki Kasuga, 16; Jack Schlossberg, 15; Izzy Rattner, 16; Will Pagano, 17, Dan Bernstein, 16; Stephen Todres, 16; and Florian Koenigsberger, 16.

15 year-old Avery Hairston is busy implementing a brilliant solution that is working right now. He and his ten closest friends started an organization called Relight NY (**relightny .com**) in order to raise money to purchase CFLs (compact fluorescent light bulbs) that they then hand out to low-income families. With the change of a bulb, Relight NY saves energy, helps folks save money on their electric bills, and spreads the word about global warming. Here's how Avery Hairston plans to change the way you think about light bulbs.

Q: *What inspired you to launch Relight NY?*

A: I saw this slideshow presented by Al Gore (this was before *An Inconvenient Truth*) that alerted me to the problem of global warming. Then one day I was reading the *New York Times* and I came across a full page ad taken out by Starbucks that said that if every reader of the *New York Times* switched just one light bulb to a CFL, it would be like taking 89,000 cars off the road because CFLs save so much energy. I realized that this was such an easy solution to such a huge problem and I thought it would be great for young people to tackle that because it was just so easy.

Q: *How did you go about starting this campaign?*

A: I talked with my mom about it first and we decided to contact JWT (an advertising agency). JWT sent me a survey and suggested that I get my friends and as many kids as possible to fill it out so that we could have some data and facts that we could use later when we were talking to companies about how teens feel about the environment. I posted the survey on Facebook and over 500 people responded in less than 30 days. It was an overwhelmingly positive survey that clearly showed that teens not only care about the environment but they also don't feel that adults are doing enough to help fight global warming and address the climate crisis.

Then I asked all of my friends if they would join on to this project. They all agreed and that's when it really escalated because just having that many kids involved in one project made corporations see that Relight NY was a real deal.

Q: *Relight NY is run by a Teen Advisory Panel. How do you decide who will do what?*

Save Your Energy

A: None of us really has a set job. It all depends on what's happening with the project at a certain time. We have a conference on our school email and we throw up different issues and ask who wants to volunteer for it. Lots of people volunteer and then we go out and do it, whether it's bulb distribution or slideshow presentations or other stuff like that.

Q: *What was your biggest obstacle?*

A: I think that our biggest obstacle was also our biggest benefit. We're kids and so we have trouble dedicating all of our time to Relight NY. We have school, school work, sports teams, and stuff like that, so it's hard to run an environmental project at the same time you're trying to run a normal life. But being a teen also helps us. We can really get our message across a lot easier... grown ups will listen to us because this is mainly going to be our problem in the future. Adults aren't going to see the effects of global warming. So when someone young stands up and says, *"Hey, you're the one who has created the problem, help us fix it,"* it's kind of powerful.

Q: *What advice do you have for other teens who are interested in launching a similar project?*

A: Get your friends together and change the way you're doing things first before you try to change other people's lifestyles and then just go out and try to make a difference. There is power in numbers.

The Green Teen

If every American swapped out just one light bulb for an Energy-Star rated CFL bulb, together we would:
— Save more than $8 billion in energy costs
— Burn 30 billion fewer pounds of coal
— Remove 2 million cars worth of greenhouse gases from the atmosphere

Get Your Parents Involved

* **Introduce Them To The Stars:** Tell your folks to look for the stars when purchasing electronics and appliances. The US Department of Energy's Energy Star (**energystar.gov**) program lists energy-efficient products in more than 50 different categories such as battery chargers, dehumidifiers, ceiling fans, dishwashers, televisions, cordless phones, computers, printers, and even windows and doors.

* **Support Renewable Energy:** If your local utility company offers you a choice, ask your folks to consider using a renewable energy such as solar, wind, low-impact hydro-electric, or geothermal to power your house. In some areas, you may also be able to purchase renewable energy credits (RECs) that offset your energy use by supporting renewable energy programs. Be sure to look for a reliable program like Green-e (**green-e.org**), a non-profit group that verifies and certifies RECs.

Save Your Energy

Sites to Surf

Alternative Energy Information **American Wind Energy Association**	windmail@awea.org **awea.org**
Solar Energy International	(970) 963-8855 sei@solarenergy.org **solarenergy.org**
Solar Living Institute	(707) 744-2017 **solarliving.org**
US Department of Energy **Energy Efficiency and Renewable Energy**	Energy Auditors **eere.energy.gov**
CHEERS **California Home Energy Rating Services**	(800) 4-CHEERS info@cheers.org **cheers.org**
RESNET **Residential Energy Services Network**	(760) 806-3448 info@natresnet.org **resnet.us**
Energy Conservation Information	Home Energy Saver **hes.lbl.gov/hes/**
Natural Resource Defense Council	(212) 727-2700 nrdcinfo@nrdc.org **nrdc.org**

US Department of Energy	1-800-dial-DOE **energy.gov**
US Environmental Protection Agency **Energy Star Program**	(888) STAR-YES **energystar.gov**

9

DON'T BE A DRIP

It might surprise you to hear that each American uses roughly 100–150 gallons of water on a daily basis. Think it's impossible? Remember, you use water for more than just quenching your thirst. Water is consumed every time you shower, bathe, use the toilet, brush your teeth, clean your clothes, wash your car, and clean your house. And tons of water is used to manufacture every item you own…from your iPod to the shirt on your back. Don't be a drip. Here's what you need to know to conserve water so that there's plenty to go around.

Top 5 Ways To Conserve Water

1 **Think Wet:** It's easy to waste water when you are not thinking about it and just as easy to save it by paying closer attention to how and when you turn on the tap. Don't let the water run while you are brushing your teeth, washing your face, or doing the dishes.

2 **Shorten Your Shower:** Get clean and get on with your day. Do your thinking, dreaming, obsessing, waking up, and singing elsewhere.

3 **Use The Can:** Don't use your toilet as a trash can. Toss tissues, dead bugs, and cigarette butts (make sure they're out) in the garbage to avoid unnecessary flushes.

4 **Look for Leaks:** Keep an eye out for water leaks and report them when you find them. Even a small leak can waste thousand of gallons of water if it doesn't get fixed.

5 **Make Every Drop Count:** Think outside the cup for ways to use the same water more than once. Stopper the tub while you take a shower and reuse the water to clean the bathroom (your folks will be shocked!); save the water you use to boil pasta or eggs, let it cool, and reuse it to water your plants; or reuse the water from the fish tank to water your garden.

Why Bother? Take a look at any globe or

world map and you'll see that the Earth is practically covered in water. So why bother conserving it? The fact is that while 70% of the earth's surface is covered in water, very little of that water is actually the fresh water that we need to drink, bathe, cook, grow crops, and manufacture products. In fact, only 3% of the Earth's water supply is fresh water and the majority of that is locked away in ice caps and glaciers. Of all the water you see on that globe, only 1% can be used for all of the world's agricultural, manufacturing, sanitation, and personal household needs.

Warming Up

If you're waiting for hot water for your shower, don't let the cold water go down the drain. Collect it with a cup or watering can to water plants or the garden or clean the tub. If you prefer baths, plug the drain before turning the water on and adjust the temperature as the tub fills up.

Gotta Leak? Not sure if the toilet at your house is leaking? Drop a little food coloring in the toilet tank (the back part). If the color seeps into the toilet bowl without flushing, tell your parents that there is a leak.

Dam It! You only need about 2 gallons of water to successfully flush your toilet (older model toilets use 7–10 gallons while newer models use 3–5). Fill a plastic water bottle with pebbles or water and place it in your toilet tank to create a "toilet dam" that cuts down on the amount of water flushed down the drain. If you have an active toilet, this can save up to 300 gallons of water each month.

Do you know how to turn off the water in your house if a pipe were to burst? Ask your folks to show you and you could save thousands of gallons of water and thousands of dollars in damage to your home in case of an emergency.

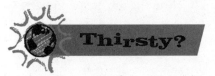

Keep a bottle or a pitcher of drinking water in the refrigerator so that you won't have to run the tap to get a cool drink.

Garbage disposals waste a ton of water. Skip it and add food scraps to your compost bin instead (see Chapter 2).

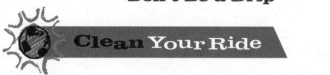

Clean Your Ride

Wash your car at a car wash instead of in your driveway to save water and energy (especially your own!). Commercial car washes use high-powered hoses and recycle wash water to maximize water conservation. If you do clean your ride at home, use a bucket of soapy water to wash followed by a quick rinse with the hose.

Get Swept Away

Use a broom instead of a hose to clean your driveways and side-walks and you'll save hundreds of gallons of water every year.

Buy Less Stuff

Did you know that water is used to make virtually every item you see on store shelves? For instance, it takes:

* 1,800 gallons to make a pair of jeans
* 1,000 gallons of water to make a loaf of bread
* 400 gallons of water to make one cotton t-shirt
* 48 gallons of water to produce 8 fluid ounces of milk

Buy less stuff and you will conserve water as effectively as shutting off your household tap.

BYOB: (Bring Your Own Bottle) Americans throw

away roughly 22 million water bottles each year, swallowing up landfill space as well as resources. And the sad truth is that bottled water is no cleaner or safer than tap. In fact, according to the Natural Resource Defense Council's four-year study on the bottled water industry, at least 25% of bottled water is actually just tap water in a bottle.[10] Bottled water is a waste! Save money and resources by carrying your own reusable bottle filled with tap water.

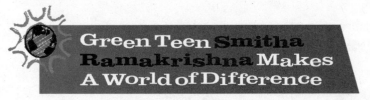

Green Teen Smitha Ramakrishna Makes A World of Difference

It was a trip she'll never forget. Five years ago, Green Teen Smitha Ramakrishna traveled with her parents to visit family in India and found living conditions that were unlike anything she'd ever seen at home. What she found most shocking was that children her own age had to walk miles for water instead of just turning on the tap. It would have been easy for Smitha to return home and go back to life as usual. But instead, she's changing the world, one village at a time.

Don't Be a Drip

Q: *What was the first trip to India like?*

A: When I was 8 years old I went to India to visit my grandparents. We were in the outskirts of Bangalore, in a town where my parents grew up, when I saw this group of kids who were my age walking to get water. I was shocked when I realized that they simply didn't have access to clean potable water and that they had to walk for miles to get even a drop of water. It struck me as very strange because back in Arizona, even though it's the desert, whenever I open the tap there are always gushes of water coming out. That trip really opened my eyes to think in a more global perspective that whatever I do here not only affects me but also affects these kids all the way across the world in India.

Q: *What did you decide to do about it?*

A: When I came home from that trip I really wanted to do something so I just called up all of my friends and asked if they wanted to get involved. We founded the ASHA kids chapter as part of the non-profit organization, ASHA For Education (an action group that supports basic education in India). And then we tried to raise money here in our community to send to India for green projects. We are now giving over 3150 kids clean, potable water and over 500 kids a meal program which is basically their only meal for the day. The money that we send over is directly used to pay for the cooks and materials to provide the meals and to pay for the reverse osmosis systems and the rainwater harvesting systems to provide the water so that children no longer have to walk miles to get a clean glass of water.

Q: *What made you think you could make a difference?*

A: When I first came home I was telling people, *"Let's go get those kids some water."* Most people thought I was a little naïve. They didn't think I could do anything about it because I was only 12 years old at the time. But my parents were really supportive and the kids and parents in my school were also really supportive. It made me realize that one kid may not be able to do everything but by getting together with lots of kids…we had 20 kids who were part of this initial effort…and by bringing all of us together it really makes our voice even more powerful. So that we can, like Mahatma Gandhi said, "Be the change we wish to see in the world."

Q: *How did you get started?*

A: I had heard of this organization called ASHA For Education that funds a bunch of different projects in India. The first thing I had to do was contact the schools in the project areas and find out what they needed. There are three project areas, two in the outskirts of Bangalore and one outside of Delhi to the north. Then I had to write a proposal about what I wanted to do and the schools had to write up a proposal about what would work for them. We had to get it all approved through ASHA For Education and then we gave them the money to fund the projects.

It's a pretty long process. But seeing the before and after picture was really amazing. I did get to go back to visit the three project areas just last year in the summer and see the difference in the communities with these water stations right next to the houses. Not only was it incredibly satisfying on a personal level, but it also gave me confidence that we, as youth, can really change the world and have an impact, even at our age.

Q: *Are you concerned at all about the water supply in the US?*

A: A year after this initial project, I founded another organization called AWAKE (Arizona Water Activists Karing For The Environment). It is focused on spreading awareness about water accessibility to all people, water sanitation, and water conservation. Living in Arizona, water conservation is a really big issue.

We recently had a petition drive to stop a group of ski resorts from putting artificial snow on the San Francisco Peaks in Northern Arizona. There were a couple of reasons that we didn't want them to do it. First of all, the San Francisco Peaks are sacred to fourteen Native American tribes and covering them with artificial snow is a sacrilege to these people. It's also really bad for the environment.

The Green Teen

The artificial snow comes from Flagstaff waste water that has gone through a reclamation process. We did some studies here in Phoenix with the same types of recycled water and we tested them for contaminants. One of the contaminants that we tested for was coliform, which is an internal waste bacteria (in other words…it comes from poop!), and the recycled water tested positive. We realized that the artificial snow is not sanitary for humans or for the plants and animals that live on or near that area. So we started a petition drive here in the Phoenix area and we got over 500 signatures. We sent that petition to the mayor of Flagstaff, the governor of Arizona, and other political leaders. The case wound up going to court, but in the end the environmentalists won!

Q: *What advice do you have for other teenagers who want to launch a project to make the world a better place?*

A: Perseverance. There are times throughout the process where you might just want to sit in a corner and play video games. But that's just not worth your time. Speak out and try to get as much support as you can. This will make your cause a lot more well-known and it will be easier to get people to join the cause because they will realize that it's a successful organization and that it's worth their time. Contact media and schools to see if they can promote it at the school level.

Don't Be a Drip

Q: *What has been the biggest obstacle you've faced in your projects?*

A: It was a little difficult at first to get a lot of people involved, especially kids because not only do you have to convince them, but you also have to convince their parents. It's a bit of a time commitment for both the kids and their parents. But I have really become passionate about this and environmental issues at large. And I've found that by showing my passion it really helps to get people motivated and get past that obstacle. Once you conquer that obstacle you can achieve so much and it is so worth it.

 Get Your Parents Involved

* **Get Gadgets:** There are a number of water-saving machines and devices that your family can use at home to slash water use. Tell your folks about the money and water saving potential of low-flow shower heads and toilets, flow restrictors, faucet aerators, tankless water heaters, and Energy-Star rated dishwashers and washing machines. Most water-saving gadgets pay back their investment by reducing water, energy, and sewer bills.

Sites to Surf

Earth 911	**earth911.org**
H2OUSE	**h2ouse.org**
Natural Resource Defense Council	(212) 727-2700 nrdcinfo@nrdc.org **nrdc.org**
US Environmental Protection Agency Energy Star Program	(888) STAR-YES **energystar.gov**
Water Conserve	**waterconserve.org**
Water—Use It Wisely	**wateruseitwisely.com**

ECO-PETS

Whether you have a dog, cat, bird, rabbit, ferret, or lizard, your pet is probably a big part of your family. So make sure that the food, toys, and bedding they get is healthy for them and easy on the planet. Here's how to minimize your pet's ecological paw print.

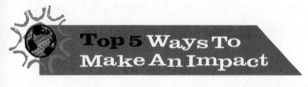

Top 5 Ways To Make An Impact

1 **Get Stuffed:** It can be hard to resist that sweet little baby bunny or kitten in the store. But animals are not toys, and they'll require years of energy, money, and time in their care and feeding. Don't buy a pet as a gift for a friend unless you are positive that they will be able to take care of it. Buy them a stuffed animal that they can love and squeeze (and forget about for days on end) instead!

2 **Adopt:** Why buy a dog or cat when you can adopt one from your local animal shelter? There are over 5,500 puppies and kittens (compared with 415 human babies) born every hour in the US. According to the Humane Society of the United States (**hsus.org**), animal shelters take in between 6–8 million dogs and cats every year, of which 3–4 million are euthanized. Check out **petfinder.com** to find your next dog, cat, bird, rabbit, or reptile friend. If you're looking for a specific breed, contact the Humane Society (see **Sites To Surf** in this chapter) to locate a purebred rescue group in your area.

3 **Spay Or Neuter:** Make sure your pet is spayed or neutered to cut back on overpopulation. These procedures also help dogs and cats live longer by eliminating the possibility of uterine, ovarian, and testicular cancer, and decreasing the incidence of prostate disease. Check with your local animal shelter to see if they offer a free or low-cost service.

4 **Seek Simple Pleasures:** Your pet will be just as happy to play with a simple, natural toy as he would be to play with an expensive plastic one. Dogs love to chase and chew sticks of any kind. Cats and rabbits might enjoy leftover boxes and bags from your holiday wrapping, pine cones from the backyard, or a paper bag.

5 **Give Kitty Some Jingle Bells:** Keep your kitty indoors to protect her overall health and that of the environment.

Cats are keen hunters and are a leading cause of death for birds, second only to habitat destruction. If your kitty loves to roam, put a bell on her collar to keep her out of mischief and give the birds a flying chance.

Why Bother? According to the Humane

Society, there are currently 73 million dogs and 90 million cats in homes across the US. It's up to you to decide how big your pet's environmental impact will be. By choosing eco-friendly options for your pet, you can make the environment safer for humans and the pets we love.

Feed 'Em The Good Stuff

Many conventional pet-food brands are made from the inedible waste from beef and poultry farms that is produced using "4-D" meat, in other words, the animals that are "Dead, Dying, Diseased, or Down (unable to stand)" when they are prepared for slaughter. How healthy would you be if you ate diseased food at every meal?

Natural and organic pet foods use higher quality meats that are raised humanely without added drugs or hormones. The foods are minimally processed and preserved with natural substances. Certified-organic pet foods must adhere to strict

USDA standards that ban pesticides, hormones, antibiotics, and artificial or genetically engineered ingredients.

Keep It Green

Look for eco-friendly gear to keep your pet healthy and happy. The boom in green gear means that you will be able to find everything from all-natural grooming supplies to pet beds made from recycled plastic.

Recycle

No matter what brand or type of food you choose to buy for your pet, it is likely that it comes in some type of can, bottle, or bag that can be recycled. Contact your local recycling center if you have any questions about the resources that can be recycled in your area.

The Scoop on Poop

Look for biodegradable poop bags to clean up doggie doo rather than plastic bags that will prevent any decomposition over the years. For cats, steer clear of traditional clumping clay litter that is made from strip-mined clay and laced with carcinogenic silica dust and sodium bentonite. These are harmful for the health of your cat as well as the rest of your family. Look for brands of non-toxic, biodegradable kitty litter at your local retailer.

Get Your Parents Involved

* **Adopt-A-Shelter:** For a fun and rewarding activity you can share with your folks, make a plan to adopt your local animal shelter. Talk to your local organization to see how everyone can help...you can all walk dogs together, raise funds, create flyers, design a website, or collect recycled newspaper to line animal cages.

Sites to Surf

Petfinder	To find an adoptable pet in your area **petfinder.com**
Pets 911	(480) 889-2640 To find your local animal shelter **pets911.com**
The Humane Society of the United States	(202) 452-1100 **hsus.org**

WHAT YOU CAN DO ABOUT DEFORESTATION

The Scoop: Trees are absolutely vital to life here on Earth. They trap carbon and other particles produced by pollution. They also provide habitat for animals and other plants, affect rainfall, prevent erosion, and help regulate the Earth's temperature. According to the United Nation's Food and Agriculture Organization (FAO), the 33 million acres of forestland that are lost annually around the globe are responsible for 20% of human-caused greenhouse gas emissions. Worldwide, deforestation is occurring at an alarming rate, particularly in tropical regions.

The Cause: Trees are cut and burned down for a number of reasons. Forests are logged to supply timber for wood and paper products, and to clear land for crops, cattle, and housing. Other causes of deforestation include mining and oil exploitation, urbanization, acid rain, and wildfires.

The Effect: Take the trees away and you've got big problems. Cutting down or burning trees releases carbon dioxide, and it also decreases the number of trees on the planet that are available to absorb carbon dioxide. This contributes to global warming, air and water pollution, a loss of biodiversity, erosion, and climatic disruption.

The Fix: One easy way to combat deforestation is to plant a tree. But you can take it one step further by making sure the choices you make in school, at the store, and on the menu don't contribute to the problem. Here's what you can do about deforestation.

1. Plant A Tree (Chapters 1, 13 and 15)

2. Go Paperless (Chapter 6)

3. Recycle (Chapter 5)

4. Buy Recycled (Chapter 1)

5. Look for FSC certification on wood and wood products (Chapter 1)

6. Hold The Beef (Chapter 2)

GREEN YOUR SCHOOL

The top priorities in most schools are test scores and costs, with very little thought given to the environmental impact of school buildings and activities. Greening your school will not only make it a hipper place to be, it will also help to improve student test scores and reduce costs.

Green schools are healthier for students and teachers, better for the environment, and cost less to operate and maintain. Green schools are also better for the community at large as they help reduce the cost of public infrastructures like energy, water, and sewage systems, improve working conditions for school employees (leading to fewer sick days), and enrich the educational environment. This section will show you how to save the planet by greening your school.

11

GREENER SCHOOL DAYS

When you add up all of the students, teachers, administrators, and custodians in schools across the country, the numbers may surprise you. Fifty-five million Americans (1 in 5) spend their day in a K-12 school. Get those 55 million people together and you've got a wide platform for environmental education and a powerful voice for change. Here's how to improve your school's eco-savvy test scores.

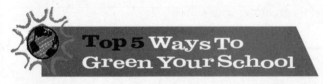

Top 5 Ways To Green Your School

1 **Start A Green Team:** Join forces with other eco-conscious students to form a Green Team that evaluates the school's environmental programs and brainstorms innovative ways to improve them. Green Team members can initiate a school recycling program, present environmental education workshops, or lobby the school board to replace existing light bulbs with energy-saving CFLs.

2 **Ban Bus Idling:** A recent Yale University study found that students who ride a school bus are exposed to up to fifteen times more particulate pollution than average.[11] Why? The answer lies in the practice of bus idling. School buses line up and wait in front of the school with the engines running; filling up with harmful particulate pollution that will stay with you throughout your ride. Bus idling wastes gas, contributes to air pollution and global warming, and is damaging to our health. Make sure your school has a policy in place to ban it.

3 **Use Paper Wisely:** Try to avoid using excess amounts of paper at school. Be sure to use all of the sheets in a notebook before starting the next one, use the double-sided feature for printers and copiers, and send text messages to friends instead of passing notes!

4 **Clean Up:** Does your school use a bucket load of chemical cleaners to clean and disinfect classrooms? If so, ask them to make a switch to eco-friendly cleaners that are better for the environment and non-toxic for the students, teachers, secretaries, and administrators, that spend their day there. Order the free guide from the Healthy Schools Campaign

called "Green Clean Schools" at **healthyschoolscampaign**
.org/campaign/green_clean_schools and pass it on to your
school administrator.

5 **Save On Supplies:** Before you head to the store to buy
new pencils, notepads, and binders for school, check to
see what's hiding in your desk drawer from last year.

Why Bother? It may be depressing to
think about, but you are currently spending about a third of
your life inside your school. And that's just in a typical school
day. Add to that any time you spend before or after school
in extra curricular activities, sporting events, club meetings
(even detention!), and it can work out to half or even more.
So it makes sense to take steps to make sure your school is a
greener, healthier, more interesting place to be.

g2g Green Tips

Ditch The Car
Walk, ride, carpool, or take public transportation to school
each day. Organize a "Walk to School" event for the next Walk
To School Day on October 8th. Check out Walk To School
(**walktoschool.org**) for ideas.

Greener School Days

Seek Out Green Supplies

Need to buy a few new supplies for school? Look for stuff that's made from recycled and non-toxic materials. Choose art supplies that are water or vegetable based. Invest in reusable products such as rechargeable batteries and refillable pens, pencils, and scotch tape. Seek out products that use the least amount of packaging. Better yet, save money and packaging by buying in bulk (go in with a friend if you won't use it all).

Borrow or Rent Sports Equipment and Instruments

The next time you want to try out a new sport, instrument, or hobby, consider renting or borrowing equipment instead of buying new stuff that might just go to waste.

Pass It On

At the end of the school year, sell or donate your extra school supplies, equipment, and books to reduce the clutter in your home and maybe add a little green to your wallet. Sell textbooks through Craigslist (**craigslist.org**) or eBay (**ebay.com**), or have a yard sale.

Get The Dirt on Pesticides

Find out how your school gets rid of bugs, rodents, and weeds, both inside and out. Encourage the use of Integrated Pest Management, a method that uses non-chemical methods to control pests. Check out the US Environmental Protection Agency's website, **epa.gov/pesticides/ipm**, to learn more.

Green Fundraising

The typical school fundraiser involves hawking unhealthy foods or environmentally damaging products that most people neither need nor want. There's no reason to toss your earth-minded values aside just to raise a few bucks for your school. Here are some great ideas for greening your next school fundraiser:

Sell Green Stuff: Greenraising (**greenraising.com**) and Lets Go Green (**letsgogreen.biz**) are just two in the latest string of organizations that offer eco-friendly fundraising opportunities. Both have a range of products to choose from such as SIGG water bottles, eco-friendly cleaning products, and recycled office supplies that can help you spread an eco-friendly message while supporting your school. Another great green option is to sell reusable grocery bags through companies such as Chico Bag (**chicobag.com**) or ReuseThisBag.com (**reusethis bag.com**). Imprint your school or club's logo on these eco-friendly bags to show off your school spirit.

Host A Green Event: Try hosting a zero-waste spaghetti dinner or pancake breakfast to raise money for your school. Hold the event in your school's cafeteria or your local fire hall and look to local businesses to donate food, reusable napkins, and compostable dishes, to make it a fun, community-building, eco-friendly event.

Greener School Days

Pledge To Be Green: Organize a walk-a-thon, a plant-a-thon, or an obstacle course and raise money through donations pledged for every lap walked, tree planted, or obstacle achieved. You get time to hang out with your friends in the fresh air, the school makes money, the planet stays green, and everyone has a blast!

Green Teen Garrett Rappazzo Puts Down Some Roots

Garrett Rappazzo wants to leave a legacy on this planet...and he wants it to be one that he'll be proud to show his kids. So he's making an effort to protect the environment, just like his dad did for him. Garrett organized an Arbor Day tree planting project at his local elementary school that helped save the planet, spread awareness about deforestation, and create a legacy. So that, one day, Green Teen Garrett Rappazzo will be able to show his kids what he did to save the planet.

Garrett Rappazzo 16, is leaving behind a legacy.

Q: *What made you decide to organize a tree planting project at your old elementary school?*

The Green Teen

A: A couple of years ago my dad took me out to his old elementary school. We looked at the trees there... most of them are pretty tall now... and my dad told me that he had planted them when he was a little kid. That was my main inspiration for the Arbor Day project, because I wanted to do something like that for my generation.

Q: *How did you get started?*

A: I decided to organize an event with the 5th grade class at my elementary school, Green Meadow Elementary. So I talked with the school principal about it and got some help from my dad with ordering the trees. On Arbor Day, me and about 100 5th graders all went out and planted trees around the school. Afterwards I gave a speech to the whole school on the importance of trees.

Q: *What was the biggest obstacle you faced in planning this event?*

A: The hardest part of this project was actually keeping things organized on the day of the planting. It was kind of chaotic. There were 100 kids running around planting all of the trees and it was hard to keep everybody organized.

Q: *What is the environmental issue that concerns you the most?*

A: Most of all it's deforestation because I think that trees are so important for so many reasons and they add to the beauty of nature.

Q: *What advice do you have for other teenagers who are interested in launching a similar project?*

A: If you have an idea that can help the environment, then my advice is to act on it and get involved because it's really needed.

Get Your School Involved

- **Go Paperless:** Encourage teachers and other school staff to go paperless whenever possible at school. Ask your teachers if they will accept assignments turned in via email or on disk instead of on paper. School announcements and meeting minutes could be distributed via email. Daily lunch menus could be printed on a chalk or dry erase board.

- **Learn Some Green:** Talk to your teachers about adding environmental issues to the curriculum. Eco-lessons are easily incorporated into science classes, math lessons, reading assignments, physical fitness tasks, or creative art activities.

- **Start an Organic Garden:** Talk to your school officials about starting an organic school garden that can provide the cafeteria with fresh herbs and vegetables while teaching students about the environment.

Sites to Surf

Green Schools Initiative	**greenschools.net**
Healthy Schools Campaign **Green Clean Schools**	(800) HSC-1810 **healthyschoolscampaign** **.org/campaign/green_** **clean_schools**
Natural Resource Defense **Council** **The Green Squad**	**nrdc.org/greensquad/** **default.htm**
Oregon Department of **Environmental Quality** **Oregon Green Schools Tools**	**deq.state.or.us/lq/** **pubs/docs/sw/Oregon** **GreenSchoolTools.pdf**
US Environmental Protection **Agency** **Clean School Bus Program**	(734) 214-4780 **epa.gov/cleanschoolbus**
Alliance to Save Energy **Green Schools Program**	**ase.org/greenschools/** **start.htm**

START A SCHOOL RECYCLING PROGRAM

Sure, it's good advice to say that you should start a recycling program at your school, but in some schools that may be easier said than done. As school budgets get tighter and tighter, school administrators are less open to new ideas...especially if they think it will cost the school money. But recycling can actually save your school money while you save the planet. Follow these steps to research, plan, fund, and propose a winning school recycling program:

Top 5 Steps To Start A School Recycling Program

1 Research It

2 Plan It

3 Present It

4 Do It

5 Advertise It

Why Bother? Recycling saves money,

protects the environment, conserves resources, creates jobs, reduces the need for new landfills, saves energy, prevents global warming, reduces pollution, and protects wildlife. In short, recycling just makes sense and starting a program at your school is a win-win situation for both your school and the planet.

Start A School Recycling Program

Research It

In order to put together a successful recycling program at your school, you'll need to do a little digging to find out what, when, and how to get started. Contact your school's trash collector, or a local recycling collection service (check your phone book) to find out what types of recycling collection programs are available in your area. If there is no collection service, find out where the nearest drop-off center is. In order to plan out a program for your school, you'll need to answer these questions:

* What items can be recycled in your area?

* What is the charge for collection and is there a contractor that offers a package deal that includes both waste and recyclables pickup?

* What price will the contractor pay for the items?

* How will the recyclables need to be separated?

* Does the contractor provide collection containers?

* What is the pickup schedule?

If you want to recycle a material but are having trouble finding a recycler where you live, check out Earth 911 (**earth911 .org**) for possible leads. Your local or state government recycling offices, the local chamber of commerce, or a local or regional recycling organization might also be able to help you develop a recycling plan for your school.

Plan It

Now that you've done your research, it's time to put your plan together. Decide what items would be best to recycle. Paper is a good place to start because it is easy to recycle and collecting it can make a huge difference to your school's trash output. According to the Environmental Protection Agency (US EPA), approximately 35% of the municipal solid waste stream (MSW) is made up of paper and paperboard products. Other items that can and should be recycled include aluminum, glass, plastics, newspaper, steel, and magazines.

Your plan should also include the number of recycling bins your school will need and where they should be located. Ideally, collection bins should be placed close to where the recyclables are generated and/or next to each trash can. That way, it's just as easy to recycle an item as it is to throw it away.

Finally, you need to figure out whether or not you will need to raise money to purchase collection bins, create signs, and initiate the recycling program. If you do, check out Chapter 11 for some easy and eco-friendly ideas. Now put all of your research and planning together into a proposal that you can present to your school administrators. Here's a sample...

PROPOSAL FOR HAPPY ACRES HIGH SCHOOL RECYCLING PROGRAM

Recycling Team Organizers
Hannah Greenleaf, Joe Smart, and Molly McEco

Overview
Recycling saves energy, conserves natural resources, reduces the need for landfill space, and protects our natural environment. Initiating a recycling program at Happy Acres High School will save money in trash collection costs, raise funds for future eco-friendly programs, improve the school's public relations, and encourage students to learn about the environment through hands-on participation. The following proposal will outline the environmental and economic benefits of a recycling program at Happy Acres High School.

What We Can Recycle

Recyclable	Collector	Payment	How Often
Paper	Recyclers R Us	.12/ream	Weekly
Aluminum	Recyclers R Us	.35/ton	Weekly
Glass	Recyclers R Us	.21/ton	Weekly

Benefits of Recycling Program

Reduced Trash Collection Costs: Last year, our school threw away XXX tons of garbage, costing the school $$$. According to the Environmental Protection Agency, the nation's waste stream is made up of paper (34%), plastics (12%), metals (8%), and glass (6%). By removing these items from our school's trash output, a recycling program will reduce garbage removal costs by roughly 60%.

Increased Revenue: A recycling program will create revenue that can be used to sustain the project and fund additional eco-friendly programs throughout the school.

Improved Community Relations: Recycling benefits our local community by reducing the need for landfill space, conserving natural resources, and protecting our natural environment.

Costs of Recycling Program

Bins: 10 Recycling Bins @ $50/bin = $500

      Weekly Collection: $45

In order to raise the funds needed to initiate our recycling program, our Recycling Team will sell eco-friendly grocery tote bags in a fundraiser expected to generate $1000. These funds will be used to purchase collection bins and materials to make signs, fund recycling contests, and initiate the recycling program.

Conclusion

A recycling program at Happy Acres High School will reduce our school's overall trash output: benefiting the environment, our local community, and our school. Initial funds will be secured through an eco-friendly fundraiser until the project is self-supported by the revenue generated by recycling. A recycling program at Happy Acres High School is a win-win situation for both our school and the planet.

Present It

It's time to present your plan to your school's principal. Don't take no for an answer. There is no reason why your school should not be recycling, so if your principal is hesitant, point out all of the ways this program will benefit your school. (Be sure to highlight the money savers!) If the answer is still no, polish your proposal and present it at the next school board meeting.

Do It

If you want your recycling program to be successful, you need to make sure that everyone in the school (students, teachers, custodians, concessionaires, volunteers, and other staff) participates. Make sure that collection bins are placed in a convenient location and that they are appropriately labeled.

Advertise It

Advertise with signs that are placed throughout the school and near all recycling bins and trash cans. Write an article for your school newspaper and send one to your local newspaper as well. Create recycling contests to get students excited about recycling. Prizes could include free pizza or a classroom party for the classroom that recycles the most each month. (Check with your principal and teachers first to decide what kind of prize would work best at your school.)

More Ways To Recycle

Check these alternative recycling ideas to supplement your initiative or to get your recycling program started.

Recycling Drives

A one time or occasional drive eliminates the need for long-term storage and requires shorter-term volunteer commitment. Decide what items to collect and where you will collect them. To hold a drive you must publicize it thoroughly and well in advance, asking families and students to save their recyclables for several weeks and to bring them to the school during a specific time. Recycling drives can be used to collect clothing, printer cartridges, computers, cell phones, electronics, and more!

Hold A Swap Meet

Instead of tossing your old books, sports equipment, and art supplies, host a swap meet where students can drop off stuff they don't want or need and pick up stuff they do. Leftover materials can be donated to a needy organization such as a library, a homeless shelter, a hospital, or a children's museum.

Sponsor a Take Back Program

Many electronics companies will "take back" old models of their products. Check out the US EPA's list of Plug-In To eCycling Partners (**epa.gov/epaoswer/osw/conserve/plugin/partners.htm**) to organize a school-wide take back event.

Organize A Yard Sale

Students, teachers, and other school staff can donate items they no longer want to a school yard sale. Staff the yard sale with volunteers and use the proceeds to fund the school's recycling program or any other green project.

Adopt a Recycling Center

Make arrangements for your school to set up an account with a local recycling center. School supporters can take their recyclables to the center and request that all proceeds go to your school's account. This is one of the easiest methods of recycling because it requires no extra storage or handling of recyclables.

The Green Teen

Get Your School Involved

* **Make Signs:** Each classroom will need its own recycling bins located near the trash cans. Enlist your teachers' help in getting students to make recycling posters and collection bin signs for their classrooms.

* **Make It Part of the Curriculum:** Talk to your teachers about the different ways that recycling can be brought up in the classroom. A science class waste audit teaches students about the items they throw away. In math class, students can learn to calculate the greenhouse gas emissions that are reduced by recycling. Art classes can help by making recycling signs or 3-D collages using materials from the recycling bin.

Sites to Surf

The Resourceful Schools Project	resourcefulschools.org/howto_script.html
US Environmental Protection Agency How To Set Up A Recycling Program	epa.gov/epawaste/conserve/rrr/rogo/program/index.htm

13

GIVE YOUR SCHOOL AN ENERGY REPORT CARD

The US Department of Energy estimates that the nation's schools spend an average of $175 per student per year on energy costs. They also estimate that 25% of this energy use occurs as a result of inefficiency. If you do the math that works out to about $44 wasted per student each year. That's money that could be better spent on education, after school programs, or eco-friendly initiatives. Give your school an "Energy Report Card" to assess energy use and help your school administrators improve the grade.

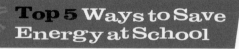

Top 5 Ways to Save Energy at School

1 Control The Temp

2 Turn Off The Lights

3 Maintain Equipment

4 Show Em The Stars

5 Install CFLs and LEDs

Why Bother?

Schools spend more money on energy bills than any other expense except personnel. Yet even though energy costs are such a huge part of a school's budget, most administrators are unaware of their monthly utility expenditures or how they could lower them. And cutting costs here not only saves the planet, it also frees up money for more important things (like better food in the cafeteria!).

Give Your School An Energy Report Card

Getting Started

On the next few pages you'll find a list of questions that you'll need to answer in order to get a better idea of the energy use and waste at your school. Don't worry if you can't find the answer to a particular question. Just move on and get answers to as many questions as you can. Make sure you get your info from more than one source...in other words, don't be afraid to ask around. Talk to administrators, teachers, secretaries, custodians, and other students to find out if the policies on paper match what's actually happening in the classrooms.

The Energy Report Card: Does Your School Make The Grade?

General Questions

1. Does your school have an energy conservation plan in place?

2. Are the school buildings in good condition?

3. What other facilities use energy on school grounds?
   Outdoor lighting?
   Lighted athletic fields?
   Trailers?
   Storage sheds?

Snack bars?
Press box?

4. What are the total annual energy costs for the school?
   Electricity?
   Heating?
   Air conditioning?
   Water heating?

5. How many hours is the school in use on weekdays?
   On weekends?
   In the summer?
   On holidays?

6. Does your school have a policy in place for reducing energy use over weekends and on holidays?

7. Is there a maintenance schedule for all energy-using systems?

Heating and Cooling

8. What kind of heating and cooling systems does your school use and when were they installed?

9. Are the heating and cooling systems maintained on a regular basis?

10. Are furnace and air conditioner filters clean?

11. Is there an air exchange system when neither the heating nor the cooling system is operating?

12. Does your school make use of passive solar heating?

13. Are vents, radiators, and cold air returns clear of blockage from furniture, draperies, or other items?

14. Is heat-producing equipment in cafeteria areas located away from cooling equipment?

15. What is the thermostat's current setting?

16. Are any windows in your school cracked or broken?

17. Windows:
    Are windows single or double-glazed?
    Can they be opened?
    Do the windows have adjustable blinds?
    Do windows and doors seal tightly, or do they leak air?
    Are windows caulked or weather-stripped to prevent air leaks?

18. Is the building well insulated?
    Walls?
    Ceilings?
    Boilers?
    Ducts?
    Pipes?

Lighting

19. What kinds of lighting are used in the school?
    Outside the school?

20. Are lights and fixtures kept clean?

21. Can lights be controlled with dimmer switches?

22. Are there automatic timers for any of the lights?

23. Are energy-efficient fluorescent lights or LED lights being used where possible?

24. Are teachers, students, and staff encouraged to turn off lights, computers, and other equipment when not in use?

Water Heating

25. What fuel is used to heat water in the school?

26. What is the current temperature setting on the water heaters?

27. Do the water heaters have timers?

28. Are flow restricters used on bathroom faucets and locker room showers?

29. Are faucets in lavatories and kitchen areas free of leaks?

Appliances and Electronics

30. How many electronic devices does your school operate?
    Computers?
    Printers?
    Copy machines?
    Other?

31. How many of these devices are Energy Star models?

32. Is there a policy in place to ensure that Energy Star appliances are purchased whenever possible?

33. Are there policies in place to ensure that all appliances and electronics are turned off when not in use?

Cafeteria and Vending Machines

34. Are refrigerator coils clean and free from obstruction?

35. Are ovens preheated or left on for extended periods throughout the day?

36. Are hood fans operated continuously or only when stoves are in use?

37. Are energy controlling devices installed on vending machines?

Pools

38. At what temperature is the pool set?

39. Is the pool kept covered when not in use?

40. Is there a policy in place to reduce the pool's temp at night and on weekends?

41. Are pool filters clean and unobstructed?

Improving the Grade

Does your school make the grade when it comes to energy consumption? Is it an energy waster or energy miser? Now that you know more about how and when your school uses energy, use the tips below to see where you can suggest improvements.

Heating and Cooling

* **Control the Temp:** Make sure your school's thermostat is set at the most energy efficient temperature possible. Many school districts set their thermostats at 68 degrees for heating and 78 degrees for cooling in classrooms. Your school may wish to consider installing programmable thermostats that automatically conserve energy at night and on weekends.

* **Maintain It:** Water heaters, lighting fixtures, appliances, computers, and heating and air conditioning units are most efficient when they are kept clean and maintained regularly. The whole school should be on the lookout for air and water leaks so that they can be repaired quickly.

* **Use The Sun:** Window films or blinds can be used to adjust the amount of heat that enters or exits the building through windows. If your school is in a sunny, hot climate, you can use window films and blinds to block solar heat and reduce overall cooling costs. In cooler areas, films and blinds can be used to reduce heat loss through windows.

Give Your School An Energy Report Card

Lighting

* **Turn Off Lights:** Schools can save anywhere from 8% to 20% of lighting energy by simply turning off lights in unoccupied rooms.[12] So spread the word among students, teachers, and staff to monitor lights and turn them off when they leave a room.

* **Install CFLS and LEDs:** Your school should install energy and money saving CFLs instead of standard incandescent bulbs. Your school can also install LED lightbulbs in exit signs to save energy and reduce lighting costs. CFL and LED light bulbs use a fraction of the energy that standard bulbs or fluorescents use and they last up to 25 times longer.

* **Keep Them Clean:** Dust and dirt can reduce energy efficiency in lighting fixtures, air conditioning units, heating vents, and refrigerator coils. The solution here is simple... get out a rag and get dusting!

* **Delamping:** Fluorescent lighting is often too bright, wasting energy and inducing headaches. Delamping is a simple process of removing one or two bulbs from a light fixture to save energy and restore lighting to more pleasing levels. The best places to consider delamping are near windows, doors and corners, over computers and televisions, and near skylights.

* **Occupancy Sensors and Timers:** Occupancy sensors and timers can be used to automatically turn lights on or off as needed. Occupancy sensors work best in rooms that are used intermittently throughout the day such as restrooms,

storage areas, and the teachers lounge. Timers can be used to turn off hall and office lights, outdoor lights, and hot water tanks.

Water Heaters

* **Tackle Leaks:** Air and water leaks waste a ton of energy. Your school should repair any leaky faucets or damaged pipes and make sure that all doors and windows seal tightly.

* **Give Em A Boost:** Your school may wish to install a booster water heater for the kitchen, where higher water temperatures are required for dishwashing.

* **Lower The Temp:** The water heater temperature should not be set any higher than 120 degrees to prevent burns and save energy.

Appliances and Electronics

* **Show Em The Stars:** Energy Star products can significantly reduce energy and water use throughout your school. Energy Star copiers use 40% less energy than standard models. And many Energy Star appliances can be programmed to "hibernate" when not in use.

Cafeterias

* **Control Vending Machines:** Vending machines use a ridiculous amount of energy. Your school can control this energy use by installing a device on vending machines that senses room temperature and powers up the machine only when

needed to keep the products cool. Many wholesalers are willing to install these controllers on their machines at no charge to the school.

Pools

* **Cover Up:** Pools are a huge energy drain, racking up annual energy costs that can exceed $20,000. If your school has a pool, make sure it is kept covered...this will save both energy and water and reduce the need for extra chemicals.

* **Watch The Temp:** The pool temperature should be carefully monitored so that it isn't heated excessively, and the temperature should be reduced at night and on the weekends.

The Final Exam

* Put all of this information together in a report card that your school can use to monitor and improve their energy consumption. Be sure to highlight the fact that reducing energy use will save the school a fortune in energy bills!

Get Your School Involved

* **Get Credit:** Ask your teacher if you can use this Energy Report Card to fulfill a class requirement...this will save you some time and energy!

* **Ask Questions:** Be sure to get everyone's input on the various ways that energy is used throughout the school. You'd be surprised at how often actual energy use in the classroom does not match the "energy plan" that's on paper.

The Green Teen

- **Teach The Teachers:** Once you get all of your information together, enlist your teachers' help in monitoring and promoting energy conservation in the classrooms.

- **Plant-A-Tree:** Talk to your teachers and school administrators about initiating a class tree planting project. The trees can be strategically located to provide shade near windows and throughout school grounds, helping to keep the school and the students cooler and make the school grounds a more appealing place to hang out.

Sites To Surf

Alliance To Save Energy Green Schools Program	ase.org/section/program/greenschl
Collaborative For High Performance Schools	chps.net
National Energy Education Development Project	need.org
US Department of Energy EnergySmart Schools Program	eere.energy.gov/buildings/energysmartschools/index.html

GREEN
YOUR LUNCH

School lunches, whether they are served in house or brought from home, can be rough on the planet. Pesticide-laden foods, mounds of energy-intensive packaging, and a mountain load of waste are a disaster for both human and environmental health. Check out these tips for making your school lunch better for your health, your taste buds, and the planet.

Top 5 Ways To Eat A Greener Lunch

1 **Make It Waste-Free:** Don't be a tosser. School lunches are responsible for mountains of trash. Learn how to make yours waste-free below. And take things one step further by campaigning to use reusable napkins, silverware, plates, and cups at your school in lieu of disposables.

2 **Pass The Beef:** It takes an enormous amount of energy, water, chemicals, and grain to make a burger. Even if you don't want to go completely vegetarian, why not make lunch your "veggie" meal of the day?

3 **Say No to Vending Machines:** Sodas and vending machine fare are not only terrible for your health; they also create waste, and use ingredients that can be harmful to the environment. Pack your own drinks and snacks in reusable containers instead.

4 **Farm-to-School:** Check out Farm-to-School (**farmto school.org**) a national program to connect schools with local farms. Your school will get access to fresh, healthy, local produce, the local farmers will get access to a new market, and you will get better, healthier selections at lunch.

5 **Compost:** Food scraps account for 12% of the waste stream in the US. A compost bin at your school can save a bundle in waste removal costs...and it can also save your school the cost of purchasing mulch for landscaping. Whether it's a large bin that the whole school uses, or a small vermi-composting bin in your classroom, composting at school can reduce waste and save money.

Why Bother?

According to the website, Waste Free Lunches (**wastefreelunches.org**), the average student's school lunch generates 67 pounds of waste per school year, most of it from food scraps and packaging. And the standard cafeteria and vending machine options are often loaded with pesticides and other chemicals, affecting both human and environmental health. Eating a greener school lunch is healthier for you and the planet.

g2g Green Tips

Solar Cooking

What better way to teach your fellow students about solar power and energy conservation than to bake them a pizza in a solar oven? Check out Solar Now (**solarnow.org/pizzabx .htm**) for the instructions to make a solar oven from a pizza box.

Get Wiggly

Vermicomposting is an excellent way to learn about ecology while turning your food scraps into usable compost. Using worms (typically red wigglers), vermicomposting processes organic food into nutrient-rich soil. You can start with a small bin (such as a 12-gallon plastic tub) and a pound of worms, or go larger if you have a large class. Check out Kids Recycle! (**kids recycle.org**) for a guide to resources on vermicomposting.

How To Make A Waste Free Lunch

It's easy to make your lunch waste-free...just think reusable instead of disposable. Keep these tips in mind the next time you're fixing your lunch:

Instead of:	Use:
Aluminum foil and plastic baggies	Reusable containers for sandwiches and sides
Paper napkins	Cloth napkins
Plastic utensils	Reusable silverware
Soda and juice bottles	Refillable drink containers
Paper lunch bags	Reusable lunchbox, tote bag, or cooler

Green Teen Caroline Hodge Schools Her School

From a young age, even before she knew what it meant to be an "environmentalist" Caroline Hodge was doing what she could to protect the planet. When she got to high school she was shocked to realize that there wasn't an environmental club, so she got together with her friends and started her own group. Two years and several popular initiatives later, Caroline has received national awards for her efforts to green Gunn High School. Here's what Green Teen Caroline Hodge has to say about spreading the eco-message.

Q: *What was your Environmental Club's most successful initiative?*

A: We've organized a lot of really successful events...especially our Earth Week events. Over the years we've had a whole slew of activities. Last year we brought hybrid vehicles that were converted to get about 100 miles per gallon onto the campus so that people could look at them and see how they worked. We had a solar cooking demonstration, sold reusable water bottles with the school logo on them, and gave away cloth bags. We also did this fundraising partnership with Green Citizen (a local electronics recycling company) that was really successful. We helped publicize the recycling event and put announcements in all of the schools in our district and we got 10% of the profits that were generated from the event.

Another successful initiative was the Green Assembly that we organized. Stanford professor and climatologist Steven Schnieder came and spoke at the school as did our town's mayor. We showed this video that we made called "Ten Simple Steps To Make Your Life More Green." It was a mandatory assembly so all 1900 students at our school had to be there.

The Green Teen

We got a really positive response from that Green Assembly and it was cool to be able to reach every single student.

Our Environmental Club also planted the seed for the Gunn Green Team, which is a group of students, parents, teachers, community members, and administrators that all get together to work on bigger environmental issues to make our school more green and sustainable.

Q: *What was the biggest obstacle you faced in greening your school?*

A: The biggest obstacle is that sometimes students aren't always as receptive as you'd hope that they would be. People just get so busy in their daily lives and unfortunately everything comes down to money. If it's not cheaper for someone to do what you're asking them to do, then they're not going to do it. All we can really do is give people information but some people are just really stubborn and they won't change even if they have all of the information. That can get really frustrating.

Q: *What advice do you have for other teens who want to green their schools?*

A: My advice to other teenagers would be to use your resources to your advantage. The reason why we could do so much at our school was because we drew upon as many different resources as we could find. For instance, when we did the

Green Your Lunch

solar cooking demonstration, one solar cooker was donated by the science department, one was made by a student, and another was donated by a local environmental organization. We also got a bunch of local businesses to donate food to us for our events. Look out for people and organizations that can help you out and ask for that help.

Q: *Do you think it's worth the time and energy it takes to try and protect the planet?*

A: It's absolutely worth getting involved. Two years ago when we started the Environmental Club, this whole environmental thing was really new to a lot of people. But there has been real visible progress and in the last two years the green movement has become more popular and mainstream. Global warming is in the newspaper and on the cover of Time magazine. I even saw an environmental type article in Seventeen magazine...I would have never expected to see anything environmentally-conscious in that magazine!

Q: *What is the environmental issue that concerns you the most?*

A: Climate change, hands down. That's the all encompassing issue that leads to everything else...it all goes back to oil and carbon emissions.

The Green Teen

Get Your School Involved

* **Offer vs. Serve:** Ask your school to use an "Offer vs. Serve" policy to reduce waste in the cafeteria. It makes sense that when students are allowed to choose which foods they want to eat, and how much they want to eat, they will make better choices and waste less food.

* **The Giveaway Table:** Talk to your school administrators about starting a "giveaway" table where kids can share their untouched, leftover food (such as whole fruit, packaged snacks, and unopened drinks), rather than toss it.

Sites to Surf

Farm to School	(323) 341-5095 **farmtoschool.org**
Local Harvest	(831) 475-8150 **localharvest.org**
Sustainable Table	(212) 991-1930 info@sustainabletable.org **sustainabletable.org**
United States Department of Agriculture (USDA) National Organic Program	(202) 720-5115 nopwebmaster@usda.gov **ams.usda.gov/nop**

WHAT YOU CAN DO ABOUT SWEATSHOPS

The Scoop: It's hard to believe that sweatshops could possibly exist today. But they do. And if you buy stuff without paying attention to where it comes from, you may unknowingly be supporting the cycle that causes them. In an effort to make cheap stuff even cheaper, sweatshops exploit workers with long hours, unfair pay, and unsafe working conditions. Sweatshops are most common in poorer countries where labor practices and health and safety violations often go unreported. But these factories have also popped up in the US, as poor immigrant workers are lured with the promise of high pay and good benefits, only to essentially become indentured servants.

The Cause: In order to stay in business, the factories and farms that produce stuff like clothing, carpets, coffee, chocolate, and bananas must compete with each other to offer the lowest possible prices. In the US, standards for fair wages and safe working conditions (generally) keep workers from being exploited. But in other countries, these standards are not always in place or enforced, making it easy for companies to exploit and even enslave workers just to supply the world market with more t-shirts and candy bars. In order to offer products at bare-bottom prices while still maximizing profits, many retailers turn a blind eye to (or even encourage) the unsafe and unfair labor practices of the companies that supply them.

The Effect: Forced overtime, low wages, worker intimidation, child labor, and physical abuses for mistakes or slow work are common practices in sweatshops. These factories are also notorious for forcing workers to labor in unsafe or even down-right dangerous working conditions. But hey, even low wages are better than none, right? Wrong.

Take, for example, the Levi's factory in Saipan where workers made just $3.05 during the same period that Levi's CEO Philip Marineau was paid $25.1 million (or $11,971 an hour) according to Sweatshop Watch. While the cost of living in Saipan is lower than in Mr. Marineau's hometown of San Francisco, these low wages ensure that employees never truly make enough to make ends meet, promoting a cycle of debt and dependence. Incidentally, Saipan is a US territory, so clothing made there can bear the "Made In The USA" label even though it is made in a city that is exempt from US federal labor laws.

The Fix: The best way to ensure that your dollars don't support sweatshops is to be very careful about the types of products you buy...and where you buy them from. Look at labels and

What You Can Do About Sweatshops

don't be afraid to ask questions. Bottom line...if the price seems too good to be true...it probably is. Here's what you can do to stop sweatshops:

1. Keep It Fair (Chapter 3)

2. Don't Get Greenwashed (Chapter 1)

3. Get Involved (Chapter 15)

4. Learn More (Chapter 15)

5. Speak Up (Chapter 15)

GREEN YOUR WORLD

O.K., now that you've greened yourself, your home, and your school; it's time to take the movement to the streets and really get involved. The point is to use your talents to protect the planet. If you're a people person, do some schmoozing to spread awareness about environmental issues. If you'd rather keep to yourself, volunteer to file, make flyers, plant trees, or build a database for a local environmental organization. Launching a green campaign, volunteering in your community, or landing a green collar job are all great ways to green your world. The info in the next section will help you learn what it takes to save this planet.

15

GET INVOLVED

It's all well and good to green yourself, but if you're going to change the masses, and really save the planet, you will need to do more than model good behavior. You don't have to yell and scream or bang on a drum. Actually, those are good ways to turn people off and ensure that they'll ignore you. You're better off making sure you know your facts and then *enticing* people to go green. Here's how:

Top 5 Ways To Get Involved

1 **Learn More:** The more you know about environmental issues, the better choices you will be able to make for yourself and the more persuasive you will be in getting others to follow suit. Surf the web, pick up a good book, or watch a movie (see below for suggestions) to arm yourself with knowledge and ideas.

Get Involved

2 **Vote or Make Sure Others Do:** If you're 18, you have the right to vote. Use it to let your voice be heard. And even if you haven't hit voting age yet, you can still speak out to make sure that environmental issues are on the ballot. Check out the environmental record of potential candidates at the League of Conservation Voters (**lcv.org**). And surf over to The Green Parent (**thegreenparent.com**) to download letters you can send to Congress asking them to make the environment a priority.

3 **Join The Club:** Become a member of your favorite environmental organization, such as the Sierra Club (**sierra club.org**), the Natural Resource Defense Council (**nrdc.org**), or the Humane Society (**hsus.org**) to support their efforts and stay informed about their latest campaigns.

4 **Give Back:** Give a little back to the environment by donating time or money to a charity that helps to protect the environment. Sponsor a local environmental club or organization or check out the Charity Navigator (**charity navigator.org**), or Idealist (**idealist.org**) to find an environmentally friendly campaign that interests you.

5 **Speak Up:** Get involved in the environmental issues that affect your family, your community, and your planet. Talk to friends about the steps they can take to save the planet. Organize a beach cleanup, electronic waste recycling event, or used clothing drop-off location. Lead a tree planting event or write an editorial letter to your local paper that highlights the importance of a particular environment initiative.

Why Bother? Why Not? If you care about this planet and want to make sure all of its plants, animals, and breathable air are around for you and your children and your children's children to enjoy, you need to get involved in the movement to protect it. If you don't do it, who will?

The Green Classics

Sand County Almanac, by Aldo Leopold

Silent Spring, by Rachel Carson

The End of Nature, by Bill McKibben

The Ecology of Commerce, by Paul Hawken

Desert Solitaire, by Edward Abbey

Deep Economy, by Bill McKibben

Down To Earth: Nature's Role In American History, by Ted Steinberg

Worldchanging: A User's Guide To The 21st Century, by Alex Steffen

Cadillac Desert: The American West and Its Disappearing Water, by Marc Reisner

Get Involved

An Inconvenient Truth: The Crisis of Global Warming,
   by Al Gore

Catch A Green Flick

Planet Earth, The Complete BBC Series

An Inconvenient Truth

Who Killed The Electric Car?

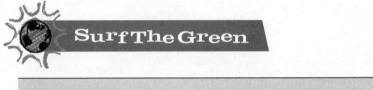

Surf The Green

Grist, Environmental News and Commentary	**grist.org**
I Buy Different	**ibuydifferent.org**
Ideal Bite	**idealbite.com**
Scorecard	**scorecard.org/index.tcl**
The Green Guide	National Geographic's guide to green living **thegreenguide.com**

The League of Conservation Voters	(202) 785-8683 See how your elected officials rate on their "National Environmental Scorecard." **lcv.org**
Treehugger	**treehugger.com**
Worldchanging	**worldchanging.com**

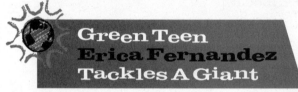

Green Teen Erica Fernandez Tackles A Giant

"I want you to envision waking up in the morning and not being able to breathe the air. What would you do? Who would you blame?"

These are the questions that Green Teen Erica Fernandez asked herself when she found out that a multinational billion-dollar company had proposed to build a liquefied natural gas (LNG) facility off the coast of her community. This facility, proposed by BHP Billiton (the world's largest mining operation) would

Erica Fernandez went up against BHP Billiton at the age of 15.

pump out a tremendous amount of air pollution that would blow over all of Southern California. The plan also included a 36 inch pipeline that was to be routed through Erica's community, ripping up viable farm land and destroying homes. Erica worried about the effect this plan would have on her family, the environment, and her future. So she worked with local organizations to educate her community and mobilize protests against the proposal. Here's how Green Teen Erica Fernandez stood up to a multinational billion-dollar corporation.

Q: *Why were you so upset about BHP Billiton's plan to build an LNG facility near your community?*

A: When I first learned about BHP Billiton's proposal, I was very concerned about my dad because he has respiratory problems and I knew this plant was going to add to the air pollution in my community and make it more difficult for people to breathe. Also, I knew that this plant would affect the environment in our area and make it so that the land was unusable even though my parents and many people in my community make a living and survive by working on the land.

My community is mainly Latinos and low-income families who work in agriculture. The pipeline was going to go through the fields and destroy some of the houses. And they weren't going to do anything about it because they didn't care if people were out of jobs. So I knew this plant would be bad for my dad's health, bad for the environment, and bad for the future.

If I didn't protect it no one else would. And if I didn't protect it there would be nothing left.

Q: *How did you go about trying to stop this project?*

A: I started by educating myself because I didn't want to go door-to-door and talk to people about stuff that I didn't really understand. So I learned everything that I could and then I just started talking to people about it…in my school and in my community.

We knocked on doors for six whole months before the first community hearing, trying to inform people about what was happening and convince them that they had to speak up. I knew that I needed to get students involved, because we were the ones whose future would really be affected. I was afraid about how the students in my community would react…I didn't think they would care…but I didn't have a choice, I needed everyone to get involved.

I organized over 300 students from my high school and those 300 students went around to talk to other people in the community and other students at nearby high schools. We were making presentations at our track meets and our soccer games. We were handing out flyers all over the place.

Our goal was to get 500 people to attend the rally to protest the LNG plant. In the end, we got over 2500 people from all ages and ethnicities to come together and we were all fighting for the same thing. This was such an unexpected victory. It showed everyone that when our community gets united we can be more powerful than a multinational billion-dollar company. It gave everyone hope and we were able to follow through.

The plan was vetoed at the California State Lands Commission Hearing and then again at the California Coastal Commission Hearing. But our fight wasn't over yet. We went on to petition to the governor and our goal was to make sure the governor voted on our side. So we sent thousands of post cards, wrote letters, and made phone calls. A month later the governor vetoed the project. That was our victory and that was when the community learned that we can make a difference when we work together.

Q: *How did it feel after you won?*

A: It's hard to explain. It opened a lot of doors for me and at the same time it has opened my eyes to the reality of what is happening in the world. I realized that my community could stand up for what we believe in. My goal was just to speak out for the voiceless and those who believe they are not represented.

Q: *What was the biggest obstacle you faced?*

A: The biggest obstacle was ignorance in my community because so many people are just not aware of what is going on. It took us a long time to convince people that they needed to speak up and show that they care about the community where they live. A lot of people were concerned about the proposal, but they were afraid. It was very hard to fight against that.

Q: *What advice do you have for other teenagers who might want to launch a similar campaign?*

A: My advice would be to speak up because if you don't speak up, no one is going to hear you.

Need some eco-info on the go? Use these text codes to get TGT info delivered straight to your phone. Text to 4-INFO (4-4636).

TEXT	For
BADCHEMS	Ingredients to avoid in personal care products
BUYORGANIC	Top 10 foods to buy organic
GREENWASH	Labels to avoid
GRNLABELS	Labels to look for
RECYCLEIT	Items you should always try to recycle

ORGANIZE A GREAT GREEN EVENT

Whether you want to raise money or raise awareness (or both) a green event is a great way to get out in your community and spread the word about environmental issues. Your event can be as simple as a local park clean-up or as intense as a weekend Eco-fest with speakers and exhibitors. Either way, make sure it's great and green with these tips:

Top 5 Ways To Organize A Green Event

1 **Set Goals:** Before you begin, take a minute to figure out just what it is you hope to accomplish with this event.

The Green Teen

Do you want to raise public awareness, get 500 signatures on a petition, generate donations, or clean-up your local park? Setting concrete goals now will help you form the rest of your strategy.

2 **Make It Fun:** No matter how much people support your project, they won't come to an event unless they think it will be worth their time. Line up some interesting speakers, show a film, serve food, plan an outdoor activity, or give away prizes to add some fun to your event and get people excited to participate.

3 **Spread the Word:** Get people talking about this event by spreading the word far and wide. Start in your circle of friends and family. Write an eye-catching press release to be sure your event gets some media attention. (See below for tips on writing a winning press release.)

4 **Recruit Volunteers:** Your event will be more successful if you can get a little help from your friends. Each volunteer you recruit will bring with them a unique set of skills and talents that can add to the success of your event.

5 **Follow Up:** Think your work is done when the event is finished? Far from it! Follow-up with media contacts, volunteers, speakers, donors, and attendees to let them know their support is appreciated and keep them in the loop about events to come.

Why Bother? A green event will get the

word out about issues that you are passionate about. It can help bolster community support, raise funds, and generate problem solving ideas. It's also a great way to bring folks together to accomplish a task and celebrate the efforts that people are making to save the planet.

Raise Some Green

Unless you plan on funding this thing on your own, it's a good idea to get a couple of sponsors on board to donate funds, products, or services. Hit up local (or national) "green" businesses, professionals, and organizations and ask for help.

Keep It Green

Don't damage your green credibility by hosting an event that's going to trash the planet. In fact, you'll probably draw a bigger crowd (and get better press coverage) if you advertise your event as "waste-free," "green" or "sustainable." In other words... no paper plates, no plastic water bottles, and no plastic bags.

Promote Your Event

In order for your event to be really great, you need people to come...so make sure they know how great it's going to be. Write a catchy press release (see below) and fax it to all of your local newspapers, magazines, and media stations. Place a notice in your community's "events" calendar and submit a listing of the event to appropriate email lists and online calendars. Locally, make signs (on recycled paper, of course) and place them in strategic locations around your school and your community.

How To Write A Winning Press Release

A well-written press release can help you publicize your event and improve your chances of success. The purpose of a press release is to give journalists all the information they need to write the story. Make it useful and interesting, and your event will get much needed press coverage. Here's how:

1. **Formatting:** Type the words "FOR IMMEDIATE RELEASE" in the top left-hand margin in all caps.

2. **Contact Info:** Insert your contact information: name, title, address, phone number, email address.

Organize A Great Green Event

3. **The Headline:** The first step in crafting a press release is to create an eye-catching headline. This is the most important piece of the press release, because if it doesn't grab the reader's attention, your press release may never be read. Center your headline just above the first line of the body of the press release.

4. **Dateline:** The first line of your press release text should include the city where the release was generated and the date the information is being released.

5. **Sell It:** Now that you've got their attention, it's time to really sell your event. Start your press release with a sentence that really highlights the importance of your event. Follow this up with one or two paragraphs that answer the 5 W's: Who? What? When? Where? Why?

6. **Wrap It Up:** Wrap up your press release with a conclusion that drives your point home and provides the reader with additional information to support your story.

7. **More Info:** The last line of your press release should direct the reader to a source where they can get more information.

8. **More Formatting:** Conclude with "###" centered at the bottom of the page.

Sample Press Release

FOR IMMEDIATE RELEASE

Contact: Jenn Greenbaum
Tel: 555-555-5555   Cell: 123-456-7890
Email: jenn@anywhere.com

GLOBAL WARMING IS COMING TO GREENTOWN

Event Scheduled to Highlight the Local Effects of Global Warming

Greentown, USA –January 1, 2009—Global warming is a worldwide phenomenon that is one of the greatest threats our planet faces today. Throughout the world, as global temperatures rise, effects are felt in the form of melting glaciers, rising sea levels, and loss of animal habitat. But the effects of global warming are not limited to the Arctic. In our own hometown of Greentown, the effects of global warming are already here.

On Saturday, January 15, 2009, Happy Acres Green Team will host an informal presentation entitled "Global Warming and Greentown," that highlights the effects of global warming that can already be felt in Greentown and effects that may occur if global warming continues unchecked.

Speakers will include Dr. Meredith Smartypants from the Institute for Global Warming and Mr. Harry History, Greentown historian.

"We all hear about the far-away effects of global warming that are happening today in the Arctic, but the residents of Greentown will be shocked to realize the effects of global warming that are occurring right under our very noses," said Molly McEco, president of the Happy Acres Green Team.

"Global Warming and Greentown" will inform our local citizens about the local effects of global warming.

For more information, please see
globalwarmingingreentown.com or
Contact: info@anywhere.com   Phone: 555-555-5555

# # #

Sites to Surf

Green Corps	(617) 426-8506
	info@greencorps.org
	greencorps.org

LAND A GREEN COLLAR JOB

If green is your passion, why not make a career of it? Green collar jobs are booming...and landing one can help you feed your soul and your wallet. The best part about greening your career is that eco-savvy jobs are popping up in almost every sector and at every income level. And these jobs require a wide range of skills, education, and experience. So whether you want to be a lawyer, an engineer, or a graphic designer, there may be a green job out there for you. Here's how to get it.

Top 5 Ways To Get A Green Job

1 **Know Your Stuff:** Pick up a book, surf the web, or talk with local experts to learn what you can about environmental issues, how they are connected, and how different jobs can help.

2 **Find Your Niche:** What are your passions, talents, interests, and experiences? Before you start your search for a green job, try to think about exactly what it is you enjoy doing, and how you can utilize these skills to save the planet.

3 **Ask Questions:** If you know what type of green job you're interested in, do a little digging to find out what you need to do to get it. Call or email folks that are currently working in those jobs and ask if they can spare a few minutes with you to answer questions about the job market.

4 **Volunteer:** Volunteer experience counts as work experience on your resume and in job interviews, especially in the green industry. And you can start volunteering at any age. So find an issue your passionate about and hook up with a local organization that's working on it. If one doesn't already exist, maybe you need to start it.

5 **Network:** Get to know people that work in your field of interest. Read and comment on eco-savvy blogs, attend green events in your area, and shake hands at professional meetings.

Why Bother? The environmental move-

ment is growing in leaps and bounds...but let's face it...the planet is far from saved. Global warming, pollution, and deforestation are still credible threats, and it will take talent, passion, and dedication from people from all walks of life to find the solutions we need.

g2g Green Tips

Learn Some Science

Even if science isn't your forte, it's good to get at least a general background in the subject so that you can understand the larger issues behind global warming, pollution, deforestation, and other environmental issues. Add a little environmental science, ecology, biology, geology, physics, or chemistry to your curriculum and you'll have a better chance at landing a great green job.

Which Green Collar Job Is Right For You?

If you think you have to be a scientist or GreenPeace activist in order to have a green job, think again. Sure those jobs can be eco-savvy, but there are opportunities in almost every career field to get a green job. The list of green collar jobs that are currently available would be pages long...but here are a few ideas.

If You Are A...	Consider These Green Jobs
Nature-Lover	Park Ranger Endangered Species Campaigner Wildlife Biologist Meterologist
Techno-Geek	Environmental Engineer Eco-Web Blogger Alternative Fuels Scientist Water Quality Specialist
Book-Worm	Environmental Lawyer Eco-Savvy Investment Manager Environmental Historian Enviro-Journalist
Free-Thinker	Eco-friendly Product Designer Alternative Health Practitioner Environmental Justice Advocate Green Living Advisor

Artistic-Genius	Green Photojournalist Eco-Graphic Designer Recycled Content Artist Eco-Savvy Interior Designer
Class Clown	Politician

Sites to Surf

Environmental Education Information	
EE Link	Comprehensive source for environmental education links. **eelink.net**
Beyond Grey Pinstripes	Database of MBA programs that incorporate sustainability. **beyondgreypinstripes.org/**
Volunteer Opportunities	
Idealist	**idealist.org**
Peace Corps	**peacecorps.gov/index.cfm**
Sierra Club	**sierraclub.org**
Student Conservation Association	**thesca.org**

Land A Green Collar Job

The Nature Conservancy	nature.org/volunteer
Environmental Job Opportunities	
Environmental Jobs and Careers	ejobs.org/
Idealist	idealist.org
Environmental Career Opportunities	ecojobs.org
Treehugger Job Board	jobs.treehugger.com/
More Info About Environmental Careers	
Green Career Tracks	greencareertracks.com
Teens for Planet Earth	teens4planetearth. com/teenslibrary/ workonthewildside/ conservationbiologist

WHAT YOU CAN DO TO SAVE THE PLANET

 1 Don't Drive

 2 Buy Less Stuff

3 Reuse and Then Recycle

 4 B.Y.O.B.

5 Install CFLs

 6 Make A Waste Free Lunch

 7 Hold The Beef

 8 Green Your School

 9 Learn More

10 Get Involved

ENDNOTES

1. Retrieved from **downtoearth.org/articles/organic_facts.htm**, on August 8, 2007.

2. Blondell, J. Epidemiology of pesticide poisonings in the United States, with special reference to occupational cases. J Occup Med. 1997;12:209-220.

3. Retrieved from **grist.org/advice/ask/2005/06/06/umbra-shaving/index.html** on August 5, 2007.

4. Retrieved from **cir-safety.org/staff_files/publist.pdf** on August 8, 2007.

5. Environmental Working Group (2003). Body Burden. Pollution in People. January 2003. Retrieved from **ewg.org/reports/bodyburden/index.php** on August 8, 2007.

6. Retrieved from **fueleconomy.gov** on July 31, 2007.

7. DeCicco, J. and F. Fung. *Global Warming on the Road: The Climate Impact of America's Automobiles*, (2006) Environmental Defense.

8. **earth911.org/recycling/plastic-bottle-recycling/plastic-bottle-recycling-facts/**

9. **eia.doe.gov/kids/energyfacts/saving/recycling/solid waste/metals.html**

10. Olson, Erik. "Bottled Water: Pure Drink or Pure Hype?" Natural Resources Defense Council, February 1999.

11. Wargo, J. Children's Exposure To Diesel Exhaust on Schoolbuses. Environment and Human Health, Inc. February 2002.

12. Pacific Gas and Electric estimates (**ase.org/uploaded_files/greenschools/School%20Energy%20Guidebook_9-04.pdf**)

ABOUT
THE AUTHOR

JENN SAVEDGE is a full-time mom, environmentalist, and author who researches and writes about the two topics that are closest to her heart: children and the environment. As a former park ranger for the National Park Service, Jenn traveled the US, learning about the environment in some this country's most breath-taking wild places. Jenn is the author of *The Green Parent: A Kid-Friendly Guide to Earth-Friendly Living* (Kedzie Press, 2008) and the blogger behind The Green Parent, thegreenparent.com. She currently resides with her husband and daughters in the Shenandoah Valley of Virginia.

If you have enjoyed *The Green Teen*, you might also enjoy other

BOOKS TO BUILD A NEW SOCIETY

Our books provide positive solutions for people who
want to make a difference. We specialize in:

Sustainable Living • Ecological Design and Planning
Natural Building & Appropriate Technology • New Forestry
Environment and Justice • Conscientious Commerce
Progressive Leadership • Resistance and Community • Nonviolence
Educational and Parenting Resources

New Society Publishers
ENVIRONMENTAL BENEFITS STATEMENT

New Society Publishers has chosen to produce this book on recycled
paper made with 100% post consumer waste, processed chlorine free,
and old growth free.

For every 5,000 books printed, New Society saves the following
resources:[1]

13	Trees
1,148	Pounds of Solid Waste
1,264	Gallons of Water
1,648	Kilowatt Hours of Electricity
2,088	Pounds of Greenhouse Gases
9	Pounds of HAPs, VOCs, and AOX Combined
3	Cubic Yards of Landfill Space

[1]Environmental benefits are calculated based on research done by the Environmental Defense Fund and other members of the Paper Task Force who study the
environmental impacts of the paper industry.

---

*For a full list of NSP's titles, please call 1-800-567-6772 or check out
our web site at:* www.newsociety.com

NEW SOCIETY PUBLISHERS